INEQUALITY AND PROGRESS

BY

GEORGE HARRIS

PROFESSOR IN ANDOVER THEOLOGICAL SEMINARY

Tout bien ou rien

The Riverside Press

BOSTON AND NEW YORK

HOUGHTON, MIFFLIN AND COMPANY

The Riverside Press, Cambridge

1897

Large Print Edition published 2013 by Skyler J. Collins.
Visit: www.skylerjcollins.com

Originally published in 1897.

ISBN-13: 978-1493566259
ISBN-10: 1493566253

To

J. A. H.

CONTENTS

INEQUALITY AND PROGRESS

I

PREFATORY

EQUALITY is a charmed word. It fascinates reformers. Prophets that watch for signs and portents as they that watch for the morning are almost unanimous in predictions of a widening social equality. When the word can no longer be used indiscriminately, it is still retained as defining an indispensable principle of progress. This and that necessary qualification may be granted; it may be smitten on either cheek with staggering blows, but it is sure to come up sanguine and smiling. It has a charmed life. If it is pushed out of the door it comes back through the window. Almost every social theory gets it in somewhere, as a fundamental condition of human welfare. A century ago there were many who advocated universal equality, by which they meant that all men should be equal in all respects. To-day there are many who advocate equalizing, not in all, but in certain respects, as the ideal state towards which society should move. They regard inequality as the chief obstacle to welfare and advancement. Against inequality the heaviest guns of reform are pointed. Progress is thought to consist chiefly in a nearer approach to political, economic, social, and intellectual equality. Even when the difficulty of realizing it is recognized, the conviction remains strong that it is desirable, and that effort should constantly be directed towards gaining the little or the much that is attainable, — the more the better, — as though there could be no question in a sane mind that inequality is in itself a source of evil.

There is undoubtedly some truth — possibly a half-truth — in an idea so persistent. But discrimination is needed in the use of a term which is capable of widely different applications, and which means much or little according to the context.

I believe that a service may be rendered by going back of various theories to certain fundamental facts of human nature and human development, and thus learning what may and what may not be taken for granted. Before social and political theories are constructed, primal truths concerning the constitution, inheritance, and differentiation of men should be recognized. It is often said that the historic sense should be cultivated by the leaders and reformers of society; that they should first understand the development of the nations through the centuries of history. It might also be said that the ethnologic and anthropologic sense should be cultivated. As knowledge of history, going back for a perspective, gives broader views which moderate expectation of sudden changes, so knowledge of the laws of human selection and inheritance, which lie beneath the movements of history, corrects theories through adjustment of facts.

The reader need not, however, be alarmed with apprehension of technical investigation and tiresome research, nor with threats of an excursion into prehistoric times. This small volume is not a scientific, a philosophical, nor an economic essay. The facts to be considered are patent to the observation of all. The method is empirical, not philosophical; illustrative, not theoretical. Science and philosophy are drawn upon so far as they serve the purposes of the discussion. Social changes which have occurred, and social programmes which are proposed, are frequently mentioned. But the book is no more nor less than a series of observations and reflections which, from various points of view, exhibit the variety and the unity of men.

I am not concerned about the applications of my conclusions to social schemes. It may be that those who cling to equality as a watchword will find support in the facts and tendencies pointed out in the following pages. It may be that some modification of theories of equality is the more natural application. But the bearing of my opinions on particular theories is only illustrative and incidental. Least of all do I undertake to construct a definite and complete programme of the coming society. Ignorance alone has confidence enough to attempt that which is possible only to omniscience. Yet certain lines can be traced down the past and into the present clearly enough to show the general direction they will probably take in the future.

The title of the book is chosen, not as a challenge exactly, but as the most convenient designation to set against certain errors which are mixed up with notions of equality, and to indicate where the emphasis of the discussion lies. If the title were expanded to define the purpose of the book precisely, it would run : inequality, a condition of progress : but that is too long a title for so small a book, and is sufficiently implied in the more general statement. Although the negative term, inequality, does not cover the positive and constructive portions of the book, it is a truthful signboard planted at the entrance of a path which will pass in due time from the lower levels of criticism to the higher levels of progress.

II

EXISTING AND EXPECTED EQUALITY

THERE is an essential equality of men which already exists. By constitution all are alike or equal in those endowments which make them human beings as distinguished from animals, as will appear more fully in the next section. In civilized countries all citizens have certain rights and privileges which have been acquired in the course of history. It is believed by many, and may be conceded, that the betterment of men hitherto has coincided with those equalizing processes which have occurred. It is also believed, but is not necessarily conceded, that further progress depends on a nearer approach to equality in certain respects.

Existing equality is commonly and conveniently defined as civil and political. That which is yet to be gained is now most frequently defined as equality of opportunity, although some expect more than that, even complete equality. This is a rather broad generalization, yet the line of division is distinct enough to be seen. On one side, the side of civil and political equality, there is the protection of law and the right to vote for rulers and measures, without any distinction of persons. On the other side, the side of opportunity, are economic, intellectual, and social conditions, and on that side there are marked distinctions of possessions, class, and culture. On the hither side of citizenship, equality exists. On the yonder side of material conditions, education and leisure for enjoyment and improvement, decided inequality exists. There are many who maintain that on that yonder side effort should be made to produce a nearer approach to equality, if not of actual possession and enjoyment, at least of opportunity to enjoy and possess.

Still further, many believe that from the vantage-ground of existing civil and political equality the opening of opportunity is to be widened. The leverage of suffrage is to be employed for prying open closed doors of privilege. In a word, democracy can and should direct its power towards those material, educational, æsthetic, and social values which are now exclusive by monopoly of the few, and should bring them within the reach of all who have the desire and the will to enjoy them. The belief is entertained that, should all doors of opportunity be opened, should those restrictions of poverty, of enforced idleness, of inadequate remuneration, and of ignorance which hold many in slavery be removed, should all men be liberated so that no opportunities of labor, skill, or knowledge are closed to them, should there be no grant of monopolies to favored individuals, should adventitious advantages of birth and culture be swept away, society would make enormous advance towards essential equality. The throwing open of all doors of opportunity would, it is imagined, so greatly diminish difference of circumstance that eventually differences of culture would be greatly reduced.

Various methods for the overthrow of barriers and the leveling of circumstance are proposed. Collective production and sharing of material goods is a method which has many advocates. Equalizing of work and of wealth would, they believe, remove the chief obstacles which now withhold from the vast majority of men opportunities of enjoyment and culture. Material goods are not regarded as an end in themselves, but only as a means to the real objects of life. Those who expend all their energy in toiling for bare subsistence are shut off from the higher values to which all men are entitled. The first step is a readjustment of the economic system, in order that all may have sufficient maintenance and sufficient leisure for gaining intellectual and æsthetic culture. Advocacy of collectivism employs argument and statistics in economic treatises, and employs imagination in the novel to exhibit the state of society under such widening of opportunity. This method will come forward for consideration a little later. It is indicated here only in order to define or at least to suggest the equality which is demanded by one school of socialists. Another school, which has already been mentioned, does not demand equal possession of material goods, but does demand equal opportunity to gain them under the incentive of obtaining thereby the higher values which are possible to the wealthy and the well to do. As a designation, social democracy is preferred to socialism or collectivism, since it suggests social more than economic values, and indicates that democracy is the power by which opportunities of all kinds can be equalized.

We must linger a moment to recognize the actual equality which has been roughly characterized as civil and political. Equal rights and equal votes are the outcome of a long process of history which cannot here be traced. If it were followed out, we should be carried back to the transition from the tribe to the State, from the tribe which was a compact whole made up of men who were not regarded as individuals having rights of their own, to the State, appearing in Greece and developed in Rome, in which there was law establishing the rights of persons as persons, and, after many vicissitudes, reappearing in the modern State, which does not, like the ancient State, consist of a central class of freemen with a penumbra of slaves, but includes all and every of the individuals who occupy its territory; we should be carried back to Judaism with its one personal God requiring the obedience of every person whether freeman or slave, and to Christianity, which recognizes all men as sons of God and as beings of immortal worth, thus stamping every man, even the lowest, with individuality and infinite worth; we should be led along the history of Christendom, and should see, even in the darkness of the Middle Ages, and even in the monastery with its emphasis on the salvation of the individual and its disregard of earthly rank and station, a prolonged insistence on the worth of every person; we should follow the course of the Protestant Reformation with its doctrine of justification by the faith of the individual; we should perceive the influence of the Church holding its belief in the value of every person, upon the State emerging into democracy. There is no dispute about all this. The essential, even the infinite worth of every individual, is the assumption of Christianity from the first until now. The inclusion of every individual and his right to protection and freedom is the assumption of democracy. To civil and political should therefore be added religious equality. Upon the latter, indeed, the former is based.

Beside this essential equality of men made in the image of God, capable of knowing him and loving him, and capable of citizenship, of self-government in national life, any other differentiations may seem of too slight importance to be regarded. Yet it is to those other differentiations still existing in society that the exigent demands of social reformers are directed. And it is to the humbler task of recognizing and estimating some of those differentiations that this brief treatise is devoted. An American freeman compared with a Roman slave has vast advantage, and seems, as he is, a very different person. Yet considerable contrast is apparent when American voters are compared with one another. A Christian, knowing God as his Father and himself as an immortal being, and realizing the law of love in his life, compared with a superstitious or skeptical pagan of antiquity, with the Brahmin longing for extinction of personal being, and with fetich worshipers of Africa, has immense advantage, and seems, as he is, a very different person. Yet considerable variations are apparent when Christians are compared with one another. The vast advantage of an American workman over a Roman slave does not obliterate the contrast between a modern wage-earner and the capitalist who employs him. The advantage of any Christian over any pagan, of an uncultivated Christian over a cultivated pagan, does not efface the difference between a Christian laborer and his Christian employer who may read the same Bible and worship in the same church, and may do so in spirit and in truth, yet otherwise are marked by wide differences of possession, culture, tastes, and enjoyments. The existence of differentiations in modern democratic Christian society upon the basis of that individuality, that citizenship, and that worth as sons of God which all men have, and which have been realized by the toil and struggle of centuries, is not in question. There are wide contrasts of intellect, taste, and culture, and of material conditions. To these our attention is turned, yes, is challenged by the demand for equality of opportunity. I would not in the least minimize them merely because in comparison with the common human nature and human rights they may seem to be of little consequence, nor because the contemporaneous are less than the historical differences of men. Indeed, it is my purpose to show that inequalities are so constitutional and persistent that the hope of progress cannot lie in the expectation of obliterating or greatly reducing them, but lies in the expectation of utilizing and harmonizing them. At all events, the differences which actually exist amongst the citizens of the modern State and amongst the children of God are the occasion of debated and debatable social theories. The demand for equality of opportunity is the demand for a reduction of some of those differences. The assumption is made that such equalizing is unquestionably the condition of human betterment and progress. Progress is believed to consist chiefly in a nearer approach to economic, social, and intellectual equality. This assumption I make bold to question. The structure of social reform is, I believe, built on the sand, if equality, in any right or intelligible meaning of the word, is the basis. I propose to show the exact opposite. I contend that inequality always has been and always will be the condition of progress. I shall argue that a state of equality would be a state of stagnation, a reversion to savagery and the tribe; that, should certain kinds of equality which are talked about and aimed at be realized, the result would be an arrest of the onward movement of society; that equality of opportunity is both impossible and undesirable; and that progress can be made only through differences and unlikenesses.

Parenthetically, it may be observed that civil and political equality exists only approximately.

A propertied man has civil rights which a man without property does not have. Even if there were no private property, the man who renders great service would have rights as to place and function to which an inefficient man would not be entitled. Political equality exists for only one sex, and under an arbitrary limit of age. A vote in Vermont is not worth as much as a vote in Indiana. It is a question whether equal suffrage should be allowed in municipal government or not. Even religious equality is potential only. Not every man realizes his worth and right as a child of God, as not every man realizes his worth and right as a citizen. But the debate is not at those points which stand on the hither side of that civil, political, and religious equality which is regarded as practically gained. The debate is on the yonder side of those differentiations which pertain to economic, social, and intellectual conditions.

III

EQUALITY BY BROAD COMPARISONS

IT is necessary now to take a point of view pretty well back, from which equality and inequality may be measured. Such equality as exists is relative only. It is some degree of likeness in contrast with a greater degree of unlikeness. Compared with animals men are alike or equal. Any man is more like any other man than any man is like any animal. The intelligent acts of a chimpanzee excite wonder, not, as Stevenson says of dancing dogs and preaching women, because it does them so well, but because it does them at all. A child capable of understanding and doing no more would be regarded as in a state of arrested development. All men are more like one another than they are like animals. The powers and qualities which men have in common distinguish them clearly from the most intelligent animals. The *genus homo* is made up of individuals who, as human, are the same in kind. The likeness or equality is perceived by comparison.

This inclusive likeness and exclusive contrast is

not as marked in comparison of the different races of men, even when the distant extremes are taken. Possibly any Englishman is more like any other Englishman than any Englishman is like any Patagonian, although the native ability of some savage chiefs and the dense stupidity of some Englishmen raises a question. There are, however, certain characteristics of race which all its members possess and which are not possessed by another race. Compared with Patagonians all Englishmen may be considered equal. It is on this ground that racial divisions are based. The classification is made differently by different ethnologists. Seven races were recognized fifty years ago, then the number was reduced to five, and now there is agreement upon three. Changed grouping shows the difficulty of clear demarcation. Still, Mongolian, Caucasian, and Ethiopian races are easily distinguished. The Chinese have characteristics which appear in every Chinaman and do not appear in any African. By common, and therefore equal, qualities of physical and intellectual constitution individuals compose a race.

But within every race, over and above the common racial characteristics, there are differentiations, the difference of degree in unlikeness from within amounting apparently to as much as the difference of kind in unlikeness from without.

The horizontal lines which divide mankind from animals below and race from race above are wide apart, and between those lines are substrata innumerable. Caucasian is a racial designation which indicates certain common features, as vertebrate is a designation which includes animals having a certain physical structure. But the difference between Matthew Arnold and a Neapolitan beggar, both Caucasians, is as great as the difference between those opposite fourfooted comicalities of nature, the kangaroo, all hind-legs, and the giraffe, all fore-legs, both vertebrates.

Nations sprung from the same racial stock are sufficiently unlike to be distinguished. All Germans are so different from all Frenchmen, or, to choose examples more nearly related by racial origin, all Germans are so different from all Englishmen that, in comparison, the members of either nation are seen to have that in common which equalizes them. But degrees of difference within a nation are greater than the differences of one nation from another. Some men of the same nation are more unlike or unequal than some men of different nations. Gladstone is more like Bismarck, unlike as they are, than Gladstone is like William Tomlinson, who can earn only two and sixpence a day. The resemblances and contrasts among civilized peoples are individual rather than national. Intelligence, culture, and energy follow stratifications which run lengthwise across and through the nations. Manners, refinements, and education trace the lines of affinity almost regardless of nationality and speech. As modern gentlemen dress alike the world over, so modern gentlemen really are alike the world over. When the uniform and the regalia which mark the soldier and the courtier are thrown aside, dress, manners, tastes, interests, draw them together. The community of scholars is intellectually denationalized. A school of artists is no longer French, Italian, German, or American, but impressionist, realistic, or idealistic. The wage-earners of England and Germany have a comradeship which bids fair to have more power than partisan and political affinities within either nation.

It is only, then, in large, comprehensive groupings that equality exists. Humanity, as a whole, is human. There is a common endowment of physical structure and form, of reason and of moral sentiments. A race, as a whole, has common characteristics, and at first sight look and seem alike. A nation, as a whole, if immigration has not been extensive, has distinctive and identical marks upon all its citizens. On a superficial glance only the likenesses are noticed. At a meeting of Norwegians in Faneuil Hall on the anniversary of the discovery of America by Leif Ericsson, a spectator said that there seemed to be one great mass of yellow hair and ruddy faces. A congregation of two thousand negroes in Savannah presented to the eye scarcely any distinctions but sex and age. But we know very well that with closer observation and with acquaintance clearly marked differences would appear. At first all Chinamen look alike, but on acquaintance prove to be different. Doubtless Americans at first seem alike to them, but they soon find, indeed, that Americans are unlike one another, that a missionary in Pekin is distinguishable from a San Francisco politician.

These comparisons have at least elicited the fact that the races themselves are radically unlike. The apostle of equality must be zealous indeed if he expects to fuse all racial characteristics in the alembic of equality. He may hope for fraternity, but only in dreams can expect homogeneity. To be of the Latin stock, — a modern Italian, Frenchman, or Spaniard — to be of the Anglo-Saxon stock, to be of the negro race, or of Chinese blood, is to have certain characteristics which are part of one's constitution, and which one cannot change any easier than the leopard can change his spots, or the Chinaman or negro his coloring. The apostles of equality, therefore, do not yet stretch their leveling line around the earth. As they would bend it unconsciously, but certainly, with the curvature of the earth, so they would deflect it in obedience to the heterogeneity and inequality of the races of men on all the face of the earth.

It is within the nations of Christendom, however, and chiefly in each of the great nations by itself, that the demand for equality is urged. It is assumed that, on the basis of civil and political equality already gained, leveling can and should proceed still farther on the yonder lines of economic, intellectual, and social rights, until remaining inequalities are either vastly reduced or become so microscopic as practically to disappear. Those who regard this as an easy task assume that the members of a nation are so essentially alike that no more is needed than certain changes of outward circumstance. Those who regard equalizing as a difficult task recognize some of the differences which have been mentioned — differences which cleave deeper than outward circumstance. My own opinion is that distinctions so radical reside in the constitution of men, that a line is therefore reached beyond which equalizing is an impossibility, and that progress consists in the realization rather than the attempted obliteration of human unlikenesses. Consequently, inquiry must be directed next to the original and various types which are found in those who are grouped together in the modern nations. The next section is occupied with consideration of types produced by social selection and by heredity, and will be followed by criticism of certain social theories which are popular, and by definite indication of the actual conditions of progress.

IV

TYPES AND SOCIAL SELECTION

AFTER all equalizations brought about by religion, by law, and by the franchise have been made, the distinct natural differences of men remain. When artificial conventions and circumstances have been abolished, the persistent, stubborn facts of inequality survive. Men are variously endowed. The differences are not in a few strata within which all persons are arranged, into three or five kinds of men, into classes of wage-earners, employers, statesmen, scholars, artists. Natural inequalities are in every stratum, in every class, in every pursuit. Persons in the same class, employment, circumstance are unlike. There are, as we say, scholars and scholars, employers and employers, workingmen and workingmen. These variations are not traceable to conditions in the past which might have been and should have been different, such as the health, occupation, and education of ancestors. Those conditions doubtless modify but do not create distinct types. Persons who have precisely the same antecedents and circumstances are unlike. If we trace back the conditions of two individuals and of their ancestors, putting in for one individual what the other had, or taking out from one what the other had not, we may believe that they would now be more nearly alike. Yet the fact remains that two brothers are as different in capacity, tastes, and talents as two men of different family and descent. The antecedents of brothers back through the generations are almost identical. The health of parents at the two periods of production may have varied, the season of the year may have changed so that the brothers were not born under the same star, the education of the children may have been slightly different, but no one supposes that the variety of types is accounted for by those infinitesimal causes. The native inequalities of men are not explained by conditions upon which human control can exert a direct influence. After study of inheritance and development, after microscopic investigation of germ-cells in the laboratory of reproduction, almost nothing is known concerning the causes which differentiate persons. Professor E. B. Wilson, who is a first-rate authority on cytology, after tracing all the transformations though which cells pass on the way from inception to new individuals in the plant, animal, and human creation, says that we cannot close our eyes to the fact " that we are utterly ignorant of the manner in which the idioplasm of the germ-cell can so respond to the play of physical forces upon it as to call forth an adaptive variation." [1] There seems to be no possibility of knowing the causes which make men unequal in important respects, so that we could modify them and produce five or ten generations hence a race of equal, identical human beings. If there was a first man he was alike. But we see no absurdity in the tradition that his first two children were unlike. If the race could be put back into the person of its first progenitor, with all the knowledge of his wisest descendant thrown in, there is no reason to believe that his children would be echoes of each other. Much less is it to be supposed that, after the mixed combinings of hundreds of centuries, men can now or ever be made alike, just because all of them sprang from a common source. As well expect in the course of a century, through processes of interbreeding, to change a mouse into an ox because both are mammalian vertebrata, and are variations from one preëxisting species.

The differentiation of individuals goes back to germ-cells which must be unlike since the results are unlike. Although analysis can go no farther back at present, even with the aid of vision magni-

[1] *The Cell in Development and Inheritance*, p. 330.

fied a thousandfold, yet results so different are capable of association with corresponding conditions in ancestry. It can thus be seen that certain causes produce certain effects, although we do not know how. These causes in heredity and also in circumstance after birth are commonly recognized as evolution through selection. At the risk of tediousness, I venture to point out some of the causes which are believed to produce human variations, in order to show that they are largely beyond the control of individuals or the enactment of laws.

It is now the opinion of anthropologists that the development of the human race depends only in a secondary degree on the struggle for existence and the survival of those who are fittest by mere strength. Two superior stages have been marked. One stage is the struggle of social groups with one another. As between tribes, peoples, or nations, warfare has been a struggle for the existence of each group. But within the group coherence and mutual helpfulness unite all the members and give strength to supplant other groups occupying the same territory. To some extent this is true also of animals. While some beasts carry on an individual solitary struggle, or at most have a single mate, and even prey upon the weaker of their own kind, nearly all animals are gregarious and find in union their strength for struggle with other groups.

There may be no conflict at all with other animal societies. Sustenance is gained and reproduction proceeds without molestation. Much has been made of this animal altruism as a simulation, at least, of human altruism.

But there is another stage of human evolution along lines of progress or of retrogression, a stage higher than the struggle of individuals for existence, higher than the struggle of groups with one another, and higher than the mutual dependence of gregariousness. This stage or method is characterized as social selection. It is a process working within each group and in the intermixture of groups. It is not a process of conflict but of combination by means chiefly of reproduction and heredity. A French professor, Monsieur de Lapouge,[1] specifies various kinds of social selection, — sexual, military, political, legal, economic, moral, and religious. For example, a Norwegian marries a German. The marriage is not for self-defense in the struggle for existence. It is determined by many circumstances which have brought the two persons together, and by personal predilections which are as little understood as they are commonly observed. The Norwegian might have married another Norwegian, the German might have chosen another German. But they marry, and

[1] *Les Sélections Sociales.* G. Vacher de Lapouge.

their children are a result of that voluntary union
which fuses the blood of two nationalities. Royalty is limited to royalty in marriage. For the
rest of the world, although custom amounts almost
to law in requiring marriage between persons of
the same social station, there is, notwithstanding, a
wide degree of freedom which is continually ex-
tending. Rank marries wealth. The English or
Italian nobleman marries the American heiress.
It was not law which prevented the judge from
marrying Maud Muller. Opposite temperaments
are united. The blue-eyed man is wedded to the
black-haired woman. Marriage unites different
nationalities, classes, and temperaments. This is
an instance of social selection which supersedes
the struggle for existence, both the personal and
the gregarious struggle. Animals mate closely
with those of their own kind. Crosses are infre-
quent even when man intervenes to produce them,
and the result is sterility. Human beings mate
variously, and some degree of contrast seems to
be favorable to fertility. Very early in the history of mankind, wives were taken from other
tribes, first by capture as trophies of the fierce
wars of struggle, then by purchase, and finally
with only the fiction of capture or purchase, sur-
viving in some of the ceremonies of marriage
among modern nations.

Social selection could be followed out in many directions, nearly all of which affect marriage and reproduction. Military selection is the mighty agency of war. The army draws off the strongest, destroys many of them, leaves the weak stay-at-homes to intermarry and produce children like themselves, and leads to the late marriage of the survivors of war, who have fewer children than those who marry young. War also reduces the number of workers, so that economic productiveness is lessened, and poverty, with its accompanying weakness and disease, is increased.

Religion has separated people of the same nation, and has limited marriage accordingly. The celibacy of the Romish priesthood withdrew superior men from marriage for several centuries. Religious persecution has killed off many of the most virile and intelligent citizens. The charity of ancient and mediæval times dumped the inefficient and diseased among the diligent and healthy, and perpetuated the existence and reproduction of the scum of society. These forms of religious selection have had an unfavorable effect. Other forms which have promoted intelligence, independence, and energy of character have had a favorable effect on whole nations.

Political selection has been detrimental, when it has put power in the hands of inferior men, and thus has imposed injurious laws and enormous exactions which impoverish millions and reduce their vitality.

The increase of the population of cities, called urban selection, draws off the best as well as the worst elements of the rural districts; mingles all sorts and conditions of men; subjects the prosperous to influences of luxury, of high pressure, and of social ambitions which discourage the increase of children; subjects the poor to overcrowding, to unsanitary conditions and to resultant vice; and tends strongly to degeneration of stock. At the same time the city develops intellectual activity, promotes social intercourse, and stimulates benevolence.

Economic selection creates healthy and unhealthy pursuits, determines the amount and quality of sustenance, and on a larger scale mingles populations by migrations due to colonization and commerce.

The results of these agencies are marshaled by Lapouge and others in voluminous statistics which show the increase of brachy-cephalic (short-headed) people, who are inferior, and the decrease of dolicho-cephalic (long-headed) people, who are superior. The vigor of ancient Greece and Rome and the expansion of the Anglo-Saxon peoples are attributed to the large proportion of dolicho-cephalic, the decadence of the modern nations of Southern Europe to the large proportion of brachycephalic persons. It is not necessary to exhibit these statistics in detail, nor to accept all the conclusions which have been drawn from them. But it is unquestionable that these various kinds of social selection, which are largely beyond the control of individuals, create and modify types, and that agencies so various signify an endless variety of types. As evidently, we cannot but be incredulous concerning superficial methods of change which are expected to obliterate types in a common equality. These subtle yet powerful agencies can be recognized in part after they have done their work, but cannot be deflected nor arrested to any great degree by the persons who are themselves the necessary consequences of these irresistible forces. Beside racial and national influences the education of this or that individual, an education directed by those who are products of the same causes, is thought by Lapouge to have only an infinitesimal effect. He takes, I think, too small account of education. The lack of such intellectual attainment and discipline as are possible to each individual is almost fatal. Education gives the increment which makes the difference between success and failure in the common environment. But he does show that other and more potent causes determine the type, and that education can, at the best, only improve the existing type to a limited degree. The same conclusion is reached respecting such economic improvement as can be accomplished by a different division of wealth and by better methods of production and distribution, for they touch intellect and native energy only on the surface. There are the types to start with. The types have been produced by causes which have been working through centuries past, and are working still in the obscure region of sexual selection and heredity and in those comminglings of population which are not controlled by the laws of States nor by the will of individuals. I shall show later that there is room for individual intelligence and action in the interests of progress, and, indeed, that the hope of progress lies in the leadership of superior persons, but, at present, I am endeavoring to show how deeply grounded the variety of human nature is.

The profound teaching of the parable of the talents declares that for every person the power of increase may double original possession. Two talents may become four; five may become ten. But with equal truth it teaches that there is original variety of endowment. The two talents may, indeed, by use become four, so that the increment is equal to the endowment, but to have ten there must be five to begin with ; and the man with two, after increment is made, has not the five with which his neighbor was originally endowed. Both were citizens with equal rights of citizenship, and both, in the application, were children of God, having the equality of infinite worth ; but in personal endowments they were as five to two. It seems unlikely that any mechanical, economic, or even educational arrangements directed upon persons who are products of obscure, diversified, and potent causes will go far towards overcoming constitutional differences. Certain evils and injustices which are due to such arrangements may be removed ; but if intelligence, energy, character, type are to be modified, it can be only by some modification of the causes which produce them. Power to affect those causes is so limited, that the types may be regarded as persistent, and even as the fulfillment of the Divine intention for mankind.

NOTE. — It is interesting to notice that a more profound and discriminating view of human development has taken the place of views which were considered very scientific one generation ago. Draper, in his *Intellectual Development of Europe*, attributed racial and national characteristics to climate, and classified peoples on isothermal lines. It is now held that climate and régime are secondary influences, compared with the various forms of social selection.

V

ECONOMIC EQUALITY A CHIMERA

ENOUGH has already been indicated concerning the inexorable facts of diversity to warrant criticism of certain theories of equality which have some currency. After the impracticability of those theories has become evident, I shall proceed from negation of equality to the positive advantage of inequality as a condition of progress. Since criticism should be fair and discriminating, this section and the three sections following are occupied with an examination of those theories of equality upon which urgent demands are based. The first theory is so crude and so incapable of adjustment to facts that it would be undeserving of notice were it not so persistently advocated. The champions of another sort of equality are as ready as the most extreme individualists to condemn this first theory. Yet it is not without earnest supporters, and is commonly, but erroneously, supposed to be the theory of all social reformers. For these reasons, therefore, it must receive such consideration as it deserves. It is the theory of economic equality. I have no hesitation in awakening prejudice against it by the suggestion of the heading that economic equality is a chimera.

A recent publication in the shape of a story which pictures realistically the conditions of life in the coming heaven on earth is an exponent of this theory. The book is entitled " Equality," and is bound in covers stamped with little rectangular blocks which are exactly alike, thus assuming and plainly declaring that some kind of equality beyond that which now exists is to convert this present Purgatorio (or rather Inferno) into Paradiso. I do not propose to follow the author into all the details of his scheme nor to point out his constant exaggeration of the evils from which men now suffer. I am well aware, also, that scientific socialists do not agree with many of his representations, and that they have taken pains to declare that Bellamyism is not socialism. But the two stories of Mr. Bellamy ("Equality" is simply a continuation of " Looking Backward ") lay down correctly the principle of scientific socialism. That principle is collective ownership and production of wealth. Socialists differ from Mr. Bellamy only about the sharing of income. He would have equal, they would have equitable sharing. Under the literal equalizing imagined in the story, all men and women are to have the same income, in the shape of an annual credit. All children presumably, though that is not mentioned, are to have equal allowances in their own or their parents' hands. No one can go beyond his credit in the government bank. If any one does not use all his income, no credit is carried forward, but he starts every year anew with the same credit which all others have. This annual credit is placed at a fabulous figure. Every individual is to have four thousand dollars a year, which, in view of public provision for many wants such as "water, light, music, news, the theatre and opera, all sorts of postal and electrical communications, transportation, and other things too numerous to detail," is equivalent to six or seven thousand dollars a year. The author does not condescend to a calculation of the total national income at such an individual rate. If the population of the United States in the year 2000 A. D. (the date chosen) is one hundred millions, certainly a moderate increase, the total product of a year would be four hundred billions of dollars, a very pretty sum to divide around every twelvemonth, with little use for it except to pay for board and clothes. However, mechanisms are so marvelously improved (the tides, as Emerson foresaw, doing man's chore for him) that production is increased a hundredfold in manufacture and fifteenfold in agriculture, so that there is an immense amount to divide. It is immaterial, however, what figures and amounts are chosen. The point is that every one is entirely free from concern about subsistence, dress, housing, and all other creature comforts, that by working half a day till the age of forty-five years, this ample provision is made, and that thus time and energy are free for culture and enjoyment. Work is reduced to a minimum, and all are living in affluence. None of the sons of Adam eat their bread in the sweat of their faces.

It is expected that this economic equalizing will go far towards intellectual and social equalizing. The picture accordingly represents a general leveling up to a table-land of uniformity above which the mountain peaks show only as little hills. To be sure, some room is left for personal variations, in style of dress and choice of studies and pursuits. The objection that independence and originality are sacrificed is noticed but not answered. The sexes are equalized, men and women dressing alike and engaging in all occupations indiscriminately. All the children are precocious, boys and girls thirteen years of age discoursing like sages about the superseded political economy of the nineteenth century. In the gymnasium scores of young men and women dashed by in a foot-race. " The thing that astonished me was the evenness of the finish.

. . . In a race of similarly unselected competitors in my day, they would have been strung along the track from the finish to the half." All differences of character, ability, and culture, are correspondingly slight.

The mere statement of this theory of mechanical equality is its sufficient refutation. Precisely what the condition of society would be if every man, woman, and child had a liberal fortune is not easily guessed. It would be quite reasonable to expect almost universal laziness, the usual result of an easy life, or a good degree of physical compulsion directed upon the lazy. In fact, the author is obliged to introduce, with the economic revolution, a great religious revival sweeping over the nation and the world, in order to convert the selfish rich and the lazy poor into industrious, ambitious, and altruistic citizens.

If there should be economic equality on any probable or possible basis, it is self-evident that the average amount of possession would be but slightly changed. Should existing wealth be divided around equally, the few in poverty would be better off, the few with enormous fortunes and large incomes would have less, but the vast majority between those extremes would have about what they have now. Five hundred dollars each would be a generous estimate of annual income. The income of a

Rothschild would give a franc to each Frenchman —an inappreciable increment. To secure the necessary product, as much toil by as many toilers would be necessary as at present, with no incentive but good will. Some compulsion would be necessary to insure sufficient labor. It would be strange if shrewd men failed to find a way of getting more than an aliquot share of the total income.

But all these theories are the stuff that dreams are made of. So moderate a subsistence as would be possible under equal sharing is a lame substitute for incentives to self-support from the possibility of bettering one's condition. Above all, since economic conditions alone have not created existing differences, but are only one expression of differences, there is no reason to expect that improved economics, without more radical changes in human nature, will obliterate those differences. Causes which lie deeper than material welfare and material destitution have made men unequal. Those causes are, to a large degree, beyond human control, and, so far as can be seen, will never cease to operate.

I am not contending that the present system of economic production and distribution is capable of no improvement. I do not deny that untoward circumstances restrain some men unjustly, that overwork and underpay withhold some from the health, the time, and the advantages, which would be conducive to welfare and improvement. It is possible, nay, more, it is practicable, so to adjust the kind, amount, and rewards of labor that large numbers of men would be heathier, happier, wiser, and better than they are. The fecundity of the earth and the facilities of production are ample to supply the needs of civilized peoples in such measure that all might have sufficient food, comfortable raiment and shelter, and a considerable margin of time for enjoyment and improvement. To hope for this is quite within the bounds of reasonable expectation, if only in view of the betterment of conditions which has made the luxuries of the last century the necessary and accustomed possession of the great majority to-day. What was denied when political economy was called the dismal science because its laws were supposed to be as unchangeable as the laws of nature is now generally recognized, namely, that economics is an ethical science, having to do with health, comfort, happiness, and morals. Certain evils of fifty years ago have been eliminated, and further improvements may be expected. These changes, however, have not been in the line of mechanical equalizing, but have been wrought by justice, humaneness, and growing intelligence. By striking at acknowledged injustices, in part through the power of democracy, and by the application of ethical principles to economic production and distribution, there will come, not the dead level of economic equality, but a larger coöperation and the constant betterment of all classes. But it is time to turn from speculations concerning an impossible economic equalizing to demands which are directed to another form of equality under the existing system as it may be modified.

VI

EQUALITY OF OPPORTUNITY: EDUCATION

ECONOMIC equality through collective production is scouted by a school of social reformers who make equality of another kind an important part of their programme. They retain the charmed word, but give it another definition. Not equal possession of wealth, but equality of opportunity is the chief condition of social welfare and progress. While they regard private property and the incentives to obtain it as indispensable, they maintain that prerogatives, monopolies, privileges, inherited possessions, and the like, exclude many from opportunities which should be unrestricted. They believe that the civil and political power of democracy should be employed to open doors that are now closed. They are of the opinion that the next task of democracy is the equalizing of opportunity, which men may then use or not use as they see fit.

Evidently this is another elastic phrase which means little or much, according to the explanation. When it is defined and qualified into the limits of the practicable, it may perhaps be convenient and available to express a real need, although the qualifications will be found to take out the equality — the very thing contended for — while, if there is no qualification, it is contrary to the facts of human nature and fatal to progress.

Napoleon said that he would open a career to talents. If some persons of talent were by birth or station debarred from certain pursuits, and those adventitious disabilities were removed, doors which had been closed would have been opened. That would have been a widening but scarcely an equalizing of opportunity. If only members of the nobility could at that time be professors in the Sorbonne (I am imagining a case) and Napoleon removed that restriction, he would have been keeping his word by opening a career to talent. But the Sorbonne faculty would have presented no opportunity to an ignoramus. Teaching in the university would not have been an equal opportunity to all Frenchmen. Had he repealed a requirement (I am still imagining a case) that only Frenchmen could be professors, he would have opened a door to Englishmen and Italians, but not to all Englishmen and Italians. The opportunity would not have been universally equal, but equal only for those who had the necessary qualifications. That is, the opportunity would be equal, other things being equal. But other things are not equal and never can be. Napoleon may have joined in the national cry of liberty, equality, fraternity, but he placed a tremendous restriction on the middle term of that high-sounding phrase when he proclaimed the more modest rôle of opening a career to talents.

Two representative examples of equal opportunity are sufficient for illustration: provision for universal education, and the opening of all pursuits. Education and employments cover the greater part of the ground. What now is meant by equality of opportunity in these two most important respects?

Education is already so generally provided in America and other countries, that, without forecasting imaginary conditions, there is no difficulty in seeing how much equality is given by that opportunity. All classes of persons are supposed to need education. The public schools, which supply this need, are open to all persons that are under a certain age. The same amount of time is given to all; the same courses are prescribed for all; the same teachers are appointed to all. The opportunity is not merely open; it is forced upon all. Even under a socialistic programme it is difficult to imagine any arrangement for providing the education which all are supposed to need more nearly equal than the existing system of public schools. Even Mr. Bellamy finds schools in the year 2000 A. D. modeled after those of the nineteenth century. All things are changed except the schools. With the advantage, then, of a case in hand, nothing need be left to conjecture. Now, the most superficial observation shows that this actual opportunity, which not only invites but constrains youth to appropriate it, is not and cannot be an equal opportunity for all. Behind fifty desks exactly alike fifty boys and girls are seated to recite a lesson prescribed to all. Could opportunity be more nearly equal for half a hundred youth? But the algebra is not an opportunity for the boy who has no turn for mathematics. He may throw his head at the book and stand dazed before the blackboard; but the science is not for him any more than the Presidency of the United States is for a tramp — perhaps not so much. Indeed, the more nearly equal the opportunity outwardly, the more unequal it is really. When the same instruction for the same number of hours a day by the same teachers is provided for fifty boys and girls, the majority have almost no opportunity at all. The bright scholars are held back by the rate possible to the average, the dull scholars are unable to keep up with the average, and only the middle section have anything like a fair opportunity. Even average scholars are discouraged because the brighter pupils accomplish their tasks so easily and never take their books home.

Educators have not solved the problem of education. Methods are frequently changed, new studies are introduced, the child mind is analyzed, and a psychological order of development made directive. Even the babies in the pre-kindergarten period must all play with round objects of certain colors. And so on, from forms to numbers, words, letters, facts, principles. New methods are continually disparaging old methods, but the fact remains that as yet a common school education does not educate. Not one child in ten after three years in the grammar school speaks grammatically. Not one boy in five, after six years of arithmetic and algebra, can work out an actual business transaction correctly. The failure lies, not in method nor in studies chiefly, but in the attempt at equalization. Methods are capable, to be sure, palpably capable of improvement. Courses of study may be too narrow or too broad. Manual training may well be added to intellectual training. The traditional curriculum assumes that all the boys are to be bookkeepers and all the girls accountants. Slight additions of botany and geology assume that the pupils are to be scientists. The fact that the great majority of the boys are to be mechanics, farmers, operatives, and day-laborers, and that the great majority of the girls are to be wives of workmen, and will have to cook, sweep, make beds, and sew, or become type-writers, saleswomen, dressmakers, and milliners, has not yet distinctly dawned on the mental horizon of educators. At a recent meeting of the National Educational Association, the committee on rural schools (which more than three quarters of all the children attend) actually proposed that instruction should be given in farming and gardening, that school gardens should be "planned and conducted, not merely to teach the pure science of botany, but also the simple principles of the applied science of agriculture and gardening." The proposition is evidently novel and startling. Nobody seems to have thought of that before. But, even if education had some sort of correspondence to future employments, it cannot educate so long as it is collective rather than selective, that is, so long as it offers the uniformity of equal opportunity. How much practical knowledge of market gardening will the thirty boys and girls of the West district gain by digging together in the school garden half an hour a day with the schoolmistress? In all branches of study the difficulty is the equalizing. There should be small groups and instruction adapted to the varying capacities of pupils. The prime necessity is inequality of opportunity in agreement with inequality of individuals. The higher education of negroes in the South is more wisely conducted than that of whites in the North. Industrial training is made as important as book-training. The announcement of Atlanta University says: "Combined with the higher education, and compulsory upon all students, is the industrial training — in carpentry, blacksmithing, lathe-work in wood and in iron, mechanical and architectural drawing, and printing, for young men ; and in cooking, sewing, dressmaking, laundry work, nursing the sick, and printing, for young women." Such education is individual. Each does his own work by himself in shop and hospital. Reform schools devote one half day to manual training, and the boys make as much progress at their books as boys in other schools who spend both sessions in study. In some of the cities and larger towns, manual training has been provided during recent years with the best results. The training is selective rather than collective, and therefore succeeds.

Education should be universal, that is, should be provided for all. But universal is not the same as equal opportunity. The uniformity of common schools is a parable which might be applied to all equalizing of opportunities for large numbers of people.

On the higher ranges of education, the inequality of equality is yet more marked. Harvard University offers equal opportunities to all. Students are received from all States of the Union and from foreign countries, from any race, any class, any family. The price of tuition is the same for all. A young man proposes to enter the Freshman class, but is refused. He expostulates, saying that he is of the proper age, has been convicted of no crime, and has the one hundred and fifty dollars in his hand. Here is the fee (fee simple indeed). But you did not have the right kind of grandfather. There is a deficiency of gray matter. You can never be a mathematician, a linguist, or a philosopher, but you will be a very good mechanic. If any who choose to do so should attack the courses and be let loose in the laboratories, if the professors should lecture and experiment before the mongrel crew, treating all alike, not one in a hundred would have any opportunity at all. As it is, after examination and selection, the chief difficulties of collegiate education are created by the massing of students in large numbers. Comparison of the ideals of English and American universities is occupied with their power to make students work and to adapt instruction to individuals. The lecture method, the tutorial method, the laboratory and seminar method are estimated from the point of view of adaptation to numbers.[1]

Small colleges are thought by many to have advantage over thronged universities, because two or three scores of men can be better taught than two or three hundred men together. Until recently the division of large classes at Yale University was made alphabetically, but is now made by grades of scholarship, for the good of the lower grades quite as much as for the good of the higher grades. Thus both common schools and colleges fail if they attempt to give equality of opportunity. They make no external discrimination, and should make none. Persons are equal so far as class, means, and family are concerned. But indiscriminate, uniform instruction is no instruction at all. The prime necessity is adaptation to the unequal abilities, the various capacities, the different predilections of students. In fact, unequal opportunities for unequal persons give a nearer approach to equality than equal opportunities for unequal persons. Offering the same opportunity to an extended number brings out inequalities. When Oxford University was open only to Churchmen, many superior men were excluded. When Nonconformists were admitted they took a good share of the prizes and fellowships, defeating those Church-

[1] "Jowett and the University Ideal," Professor W. J. Ashley: *The Atlantic Monthly*, July, 1897.

men who otherwise would have succeeded. The wider competition and selection emphasized inequality, as equalizing of opportunity always does.

Education is an unfortunate example for the advocates of equality of opportunity. They would be more consistent if they demanded unequal opportunity, since that would make the most rather than the least of those who are inferior. Let everybody go to school, by all means, and in that respect be equal to every other body. But let the opportunities in the schools be as unequal as the persons and as their future vocations. Professor Paulsen, of Berlin, shows that the educational ideal has been tending towards individuality so that each may be taught according to his natural endowment, and has been moving away from uniformity by introducing natural science, history, and industrial training. He says that the ideal is "vigor and originality, not equality, nor that uniformity which disregards the demands of nature; for this produces weakness and false culture. Let us extend to every individual the liberty of developing his talents according to the demands of his nature, in order that he may reach the summit of his capacity."[1] In this sense culture may and should be universal. There should be no illiteracy. There should be a suitable education for all.

[1] "The Evolution of the Educational Ideal," *The Forum*, August, 1897.

VII

EQUALITY OF OPPORTUNITY : PURSUITS

THE other demand is for equality in pursuits, occupations, and professions. The complaint is heard that occupations which are open to some are closed to others, and it is maintained that all occupations should be equally open to all persons. It is believed that equal freedom to enter any and all pursuits would greatly relieve the strain of hardship and poverty by increase of wages, salaries, and incomes, and so would put men in the way of obtaining comfort, enjoyment, and culture. What, now, is the nature, and what the reasonableness of this demand ? The nature of the demand is perceived by noticing the causes which are supposed to debar many persons from certain pursuits.

Want of capital is one cause. Every productive business requires capital. A man without capital or without credit to obtain it cannot become a woolen manufacturer. Another cause is want of influence. The sons of capitalists and manufacturers are provided with occupation by their fathers. A professional man induces a merchant who is his client, or patient, or parishioner, to employ his son on a salary with prospect of a small interest in the business. Favoritism thus opens pursuits to some and thereby closes them to others. It is claimed that such opportunities should be equally open to all. Another cause which makes opportunities unequal is the combination of capital in vast amounts held by corporations, trusts, and syndicates which crowd out or buy out small manufacturers. Still another cause is lack of training. Men without education cannot be physicians, lawyers, preachers, teachers, editors, architects, musicians, and artists. The only pursuits open to those who have no capital, no influence, or no education, are the wage-earning pursuits in manufacture and agriculture, or, at the best, positions as foremen and overseers in shops or mills, and ownership of small farms.

The opening of pursuits which require capital is possible only by a radical change in the economic system. The only system under which there can be equality of opportunity is collective production, which is not desired by the advocates of equal opportunity. And if that system were adopted, the majority would be laborers under direction. Even the economic army of socialism cannot be composed entirely of major-generals. It is expected, indeed, that there would not be as many managers as now. There would be only a different method of rewarding the rank and file, who would have the very same pursuits they are now engaged in.

Something might be done to limit the amount of capital a corporation can hold, and so increase the number of manufacturers. Trusts and syndicates might be forbidden by law. There are laws on the statute-books to prevent the restraint of trade, and these laws might be rigidly enforced. But considerable massing of capital is essential to cheapness of production. Small factories increase the price of commodities; large factories and department stores cheapen prices. Trusts and syndicates are exposed to competition, and thus far only a few of them have been successful. So long as private enterprise using private capital is permitted, so long the number who are engaged in business for profit must be relatively small. Nothing more is to be desired than that the savings of industry may find investment in profitable business, as they now do by millions of dollars deposited in banks and invested in stocks, and that thrifty men may be able to set up in business for themselves, as they are constantly doing. Possibly such use of savings can be made easier by legislation, and, if that is equality of opportunity, everybody is in favor of it.

Profit-sharing, if it should become generally

practicable, would give industrious and skillful workmen a share of the gains and a voice in the conduct of business, but would not give opportunity to all to become managers.

As to the advantage of favored sons, a good deal could be said for permanence and continuity of management thus secured. As yet, however, instances of such continuity for three or four generations are rare. There are not sons and grandsons enough in some families, or, indeed, all the boys are girls, or there are no children at all, or the sons prefer intellectual pursuits, even if they are not content to live in elegant leisure on allowance and inherited income, or inefficient sons are crowded out by more enterprising men. Since charity has become the fashion, poor boys of promise find positions more easily than the sons of professional men. Protégés are more interesting than social equals.

An extension of municipal ownership and management is advocated as one way of enlarging opportunity, by opening a great number of positions. If the government is pure, some capable men will be transferred from private to public employments, but the number of occupations will not be increased, nor will incapable men obtain positions. If the government is not pure, favoritism and corruption will limit opportunity, and will be as much inveighed against as capital and family interest are now. The evils of French bureaucracy would be upon us in full force. Municipal provision of enjoyments and facilities, such as parks, museums, libraries, and baths, is not for the purpose of opening pursuits, but of promoting the comfort and culture of all citizens, whatever their pursuits. As to public ownership and control which stop short of collectivism, there is a necessary and rather narrow limit in the nature of the case, for they are dependent on taxation, that is, on a portion of the earnings and incomes of individual industry. Should public be as extensive as private ownership, half and half, it is obvious that the half of private income would be taken by the tax-gatherer, and that the people would not have enough left to provide the necessaries of life. They would go without bread in order to have a pleasant park to sit in. Half ownership by city, State, and nation would have to be whole ownership, and we are landed again in universal collectivism. But by the assumption, collectivism is not demanded, and so public control can open but few opportunities.

If the existing system is not to be essentially changed, if the community is not to go over to collectivism, reliance must be placed on training and education for equality of opportunity. Let no man be debarred from as complete an education as he can acquire, so that all may be fitted for appropriate pursuits. This conclusion carries us back to what has already been said concerning education. Statistics show that only a small percentage of pupils — about five per centum — pass beyond the grammar schools. A reason alleged is the necessity of going to work. It is assumed that, if the education were carried further, if all went through the high school and the scientific or academic schools, they would not be condemned to the position of wage-earners, or at least not so many of them. It is true that some children are taken out of school by their parents in order that they may work and help support the family. But I believe that very few bright and promising pupils are thus arrested in the course of education. They are incited by teachers to go on, and their parents desire them to go on. The fact is that the vast majority do not wish to study. They are not very intelligent, they tire of school, they wish to be earning money for themselves. Young persons leave school because they can engage in occupations which they have enough fitness to pursue. The assumption in question furnishes, then, this interesting conclusion: pursuits are not open because young men and women are not sufficiently educated; young men and women leave school early in order to engage in lucrative pursuits. The high schools are depleted by the inducements of waiting occupations, but persons do not have occupations because they do not attend the high school. The real reason education is arrested is not objective, but subjective. It is not because circumstances prevent attendance, nor because schools are wanting, but because young persons prefer work to study. Few American boys that thirst for knowledge are forced out of school into the mill. My own opinion is that it is a great deal better for the most of the pupils not to remain in school. They are cut out for mechanics, weavers, farmers, artisans. To acquire skill in their pursuits they should begin early. A musician said that he could never be a really great pianist because he did not begin till he was twenty years of age. The hand must be developed during the period of growth if one is to be a master. This is equally true of nearly all occupations which require physical skill. Also, by beginning manual work early proper provision can be made for marriage. Above all, the higher schools do not fit scholars, but actually unfit them, for manual pursuits, by giving a smattering of knowledge and by creating distaste for the humble tasks to which the majority are best suited. Some allowance being made for untoward circumstances, — an allowance which must be made until at some distant day society comes to perfection, — the real reason why the vast majority work with their hands the thing that is good, and the small minority work with their brains the thing that is good, the real reason why the higher pursuits are not open to all, is the persons themselves. The personal equation chiefly determines occupation and remuneration. A few are capable of directing others; the many need direction.

Too much opportunity is lack of opportunity. An easy path invites sauntering. A steep path compels climbing. On the other hand, lack of opportunity may become opportunity. Strong purpose creates opportunity. The very making of opportunity out of nothing is itself the best possible opportunity. A poor Italian boy, at school in an American city, has musical talent. He picks up tunes by ear and plays the piano when there is singing in the school. The teacher speaks of him to a wealthy woman, who sends him to a musical instructor. The boy makes rapid progress. He practices four hours a day besides attending school five hours. He lives in a home barely raised above poverty. Music is the chief interest, the consuming passion, always a change for the better from home and school. Another boy in better circumstances has as much musical talent. He is put under an instructor and makes considerable progress. But the chances are that he will not be as fine a pianist as the Italian, because he has other real interests — reading, studies, society, amusements. Above all, he has no such spur of necessity as the other, to whom music means a livelihood and a career. The boy who has every opportunity may become a better educated and more cultivated man than the other, but is not as likely to become a great musician. It may be said that the teacher and the wealthy woman gave the Italian an opportunity which other poor boys of talent do not have, and that this opportunity is the very thing contended for, that many poor boys might be fine musicians if they had such opportunity. So, it is said, there may be potential scholars, lawyers, preachers, merchants, and organizers, who would be preëminent in the higher pursuits if the teacher and rich patroness should be raised up to give them opportunity. Nobody knows how many mute, inglorious Miltons are buried alive in shops and cotton mills before they are finally buried in country churchyards. This is more than doubtful. Their teachers do point out promising pupils and encourage them. Their own ambitions push them on. Their parents are ambitious for them. With rare exceptions they find or create opportunities, and by the very effort necessary for making their way, are developed in character and talent as they might not be if the doors of opportunity were held open for them, and they were kindly pushed along the line of least resistance rather than obliged to push themselves along the line of greatest resistance. Ten to one the Italian would become a professional musician of some kind, patroness or no patroness. Necessity is often a better friend than opportunity. The accident of poverty compelled George Eliot to write her first story, " Amos Barton." The great books and great musical compositions have come as often from men compelled by the pressure of necessity to put their best energies into their work as from those under no other pressure than ambition. The difference between superlative and comparative success has often been the difference between the opportunity of compulsion and the opportunity of ease. Some of Mendelssohn's admirers think that he would have taken higher rank as a composer if, instead of having every advantage, he had been as poor as other composers whose life was a struggle, but who surpassed him.

The assumption that there would be many more persons than there are in the higher pursuits, if opportunity were opened, is questionable. There are only a few higher places, and, correspondingly, there are only a few who have ability to fill higher places. A hundred mechanics are needed where one employer is needed. It is as important that those who are capable of being good workmen should be trained for mechanical pursuits as that those who are capable of organization should be trained for that. The notion that a large number of young men should aspire to high positions has overcrowded the learned professions in Germany, America, and other countries with men who are doomed to failure in those professions, not so much by reason of the overcrowding as by reason of unfitness, but who would succeed in manual pursuits.

I am not maintaining that every one has a suitable opportunity. The adjustments of society are not yet perfect. I am only claiming that external opportunity has but a small part in the conditions of success, and that, on the whole, persons of character, ability, and energy do find or make opportunities by which they rise to their proper level in the economic, professional, and social scale. I have also hinted that opportunity made easy may be an actual hindrance to success.

There is yet another form of the demand for equality of opportunity. It is a demand for opportunities of enjoyment and culture for those who are engaged in the various pursuits of life. There should be public libraries, museums, parks, roads, baths, theatres, concerts, and so forth. But this is merely to define the proper object of good government. Wants which are general and can be supplied better by concerted than by individual action should be provided for by the municipality or the State. Some of these wants are so nearly universal that municipalities are not only permitted but required by law to supply them. These public functions, of which there will probably and properly be further extension, are mentioned here only for the purpose of observing that they do not promote equal opportunities. Schools, universities, libraries, galleries, operas, and circuses may yet be open to all, but they will not be really open for those who cannot appreciate them. Picture-galleries are no opportunity to a blind man, nor to a man æsthetically blind. Symphonies are no opportunity to a deaf man, nor to a man æsthetically deaf. Universities are no opportunity to a dull man, nor bull-fights to a refined man. Even if all wealth were possessed by the community and public provision were made for all wants, there could be no equality. Valuable books might be wanted by only one man. To provide them for him would be unjust, for accumulated wealth would be limited, and money would have to be taken from the common store to endow libraries, leaving too little for the prize-fights, circuses, and bicycles, which the majority would prefer.

Opportunities can be equal only if men are equal. Men are not equal now and can never be made equal. At the best, some obstructing mechanisms can be removed. The partitions which divide a railway carriage into first, second, and third class compartments may be knocked out, and the seats and fares made uniform, but the vender of books and magazines, to drive a brisk trade, must still offer a considerable variety.

What, now, is the use of talking about equality of opportunity under any economic or political system? A mouse and an ox may be in the same field, ranging over the same area, but the roots are no opportunity for the ox, and the grass is no opportunity for the mouse. Neither can education, pursuits, and public provision for comforts and enjoyments be equal opportunities for unequal persons.

VIII

A FAIR CHANCE

BUT what is really meant, it may be said, is not a literal equality of opportunity which will create equal men, for no one is fool enough to suppose that possible. What is meant is, for every man a fair chance, so that nothing shall stand in the way of his making the most of himself and the best of his powers. But that is a very different proposition from equality of opportunity, taken literally or taken in any intelligible meaning. For every man a fair chance means a chance of which this or that man can avail himself, — a fair chance for *him*. This is the exact converse of equality of opportunity. A fair chance for one man is no chance at all for another. There is no chance which is equally fair for any two men on earth. A fair chance is a suitable opportunity, such that one may do what he is fitted to do, may learn that which is useful to him, and may attain all the self-improvement possible. Fair is a word which means just and right and fitting. It means correspondence of circumstance to person. It recognizes the variety of human powers and capacities. It is the correlative of inequality rather than the synonym of equality. It is not fair to an illiterate man to elect him chairman of the school committee. It puts him at an enormous disadvantage and exposes him to ridicule. It is not fair to a philosopher to keep him on a shoemaker's bench, spite of the case of Boehme, nor is it fair to others. It spoils a good thinker to make a poor shoemaker, as conversely many a good carpenter is spoiled to make a poor preacher. *Sutor ne supra crepidam judicaret.* " Blessed is the man who has found his work." And blessed is the born shoemaker who has found and who sticks to his last. That is the only fair chance for him. Surely he has not an equal opportunity with a statesman, although he has just as fair a chance.

The admission of those who demand a nearer approach to equality does not, in fact, go so far as the fair chance theory goes. They really believe, after all, that the chances which are appropriate tend to make men equal; that, if all had fair chances, the effect would be leveling up and leveling down ; and that, with the disappearance of extremes in material conditions would disappear also, to a considerable degree, the intellectual differences of men. This conclusion is more than doubtful. The widening of opportunity and the betterment

of material circumstances which have occurred,
and even the education which has become so
general that illiteracy scarcely exists in some
countries, have not appreciably reduced native
differences, have, in fact, accentuated unlikeness.
Outward and material equality and external opportunity of education emphasize intellectual, æsthetic,
and moral differences, and give the verbal paradox of the inequality of equality. Even Bellamy
has an inkling of this paradox, and sacrifices his
central principle to meet one of the most forcible
objections to socialism. He says that differences
of height are most apparent when men stand on
level ground, that economic equality is the leveling
of the ground which brings out the natural inequalities of men. It did not occur to him that on un-
even ground the tall men gain the eminences and
the little men are pushed into the hollows, and
that on the same level such accidental variations
would disappear. But his illustration, spite of
himself, tells against his philosophy of equality.
Thus, equality of opportunity, even when it is
translated into fair chance, is a counter, a catch-
word, which merely means that so far as men are
equal, opportunities should be equal. But the
very equalizing of opportunity, as in schools, libraries, museums, and all that provides for the intellectual man, only shows how unequal men are, that

groups of equal men are very small and therefore very numerous, in fact throws us back with increased force upon the endless variety of individual differences which proceed from the thousand obscure yet potent causes that have produced a human race so diversified that no two men can be found who are precisely alike. It has been as wittily as sagaciously observed that the differences between men are not very great, but that what difference there is amounts to a great deal. Asa Gray applied this to the difference between man and the erect animal most nearly like man. The resemblances are great, but the differences, slight as they may seem, amount to a great deal, amount, in fact, to more than the resemblances.

Stevenson, with characteristic insight and humor, asking what constitutes a gentleman, reverts to causes which lie back of the individual and of his personal culture. He says that the ancient and stupid belief that to belong to a good family makes one a gentleman implies a modern scientific theory. What he says should be repeated in his own inimitable style: " The ancient and stupid belief came to the ground with a prodigious dust and the collapse of several polities, in the latter half of the last century. There followed upon this an interregnum, during which it was believed that all men were born 'free and equal,' and it really did not matter who your father was. Man has always been so nobly irrational, bandaging his eyes against the facts of life, feeding himself on the wind of ambitious falsehood, counting his stock to be the children of the gods ; and yet perhaps he never showed in a more touching light than when he embraced this boyish theory. . . . And the ancient stupid belief having come to the ground and the dust of its fall subsided, behold the modern scientific theory beginning to rise very nearly on the old foundation, and individuals no longer (as was fondly imagined) springing into life from God knows where, incalculable, untrammeled, abstract, equal to one another — but issuing modestly from a race, with virtues and vices, fortitudes and frailties, ready made ; the slaves of their inheritance of blood ; eternally unequal. So that we in the present, and yet more our scientific descendants in the future, must use, when we desire to praise a character, the old expression, gentleman, in nearly the old sense ; one of a happy strain of blood, one fortunate in descent from brave and self-respecting ancestors, whether clowns or counts." [1]

The various kinds of equality which find advocates have been tracked down to their self-contradictions and elusiveness, partly because they seem to many to mark the direction of progress, and

[1] Essay on Gentlemen.

partly to show the path along which the real onward ascent of men must slowly travel.   The inevitable facts have been pointed out, not merely that
the inevitable may be accepted rather than fought
against, but that the positive advantage of inequality may be recognized and utilized.   Negative criticism of untenable theories therefore gives place,
through the remainder of this essay, to positive
construction.

NOTE. — Poverty presents a problem which lies outside
the range of this discussion.   Its causes lie chiefly in in-
competence, lack of energy, bad heredity, and unhealthy
surroundings, rather than in a vicious economic system, or
in lack of opportunity.   The relief of poverty has become so
judicious that few poor persons are left to suffer from want.
The prevention of poverty is to be found in good sanitation
enforced by the municipality, in suitable education of individuals according to capacity, and in self-help, rather than
in economic revolutions or in indiscriminate equality of opportunity.

IX

INEQUALITY is not the only, nor, for most purposes, the best word to express the native and acquired unlikenesses of men. It is a negative word, signifying the absence of equality, but affirming nothing. For that matter equality affirms nothing. It is the connecting link $(=)$ between two members of an equation, but the link which means "equal to" does not say whether it stands between tons of iron or bushels of wheat, whether it balances cattle or men in the level scale. I have used the negative designation freely because it is a more emphatic denial of popular theories than any other, because it is the only word which meets equality on its own ground. But as I now attempt to put something into the two sides of the scale, the something which makes one side ascend and the other side descend, I introduce words which have some positive significance. Equality and inequality are comparisons of things which are capable of quantitative measurement and weighing. They cannot be applied exactly to intellectual qualities nor to any of the higher forms of human energy. Power to lift weights can be measured exactly. One man, in that respect, is equal or unequal to another. So running two hundred feet or vaulting over a bar is equal or unequal. Skill is less capable of measurement, except in producing mechanical results, such as the number of yards of cloth different persons can take through two looms in a day. Beyond muscular strength and skill producing physical results, quantitative measurements are not possible. Resort must be taken to indefinite comparisons, expressed by the words, superior and inferior, higher and lower, better and worse, better and best. Even these terms are inexact and sometimes invidious. There is, however, one word which can give no offense, the word " variety ; " and it will now be used to indicate the differing characteristics, capabilities, and attainments of men, although the other terms will also be employed for purposes of comparison.

Society is often compared to an organism, or even is regarded as a true organism. This comparison or representation is employed to illustrate the variety and coördination of interrelated functions. Some writers debate warmly the question whether society is an organism or not. Into that debate we need not enter. At the most, I think a vital organism is only a simile. It may be held that society is like an organism, but not that society *is* an organism. Even as a figure, it does not apply in all respects, for figures and similes never do. The likeness fails, especially in respect to self-consciousness. A living organism of many members has one central self-consciousness, or, indeed, as in the case of plants, may have no consciousness at all. Animals and men have one consciousness conditioned on the mutual action and reaction of the members. In the social organism each member has his own consciousness, but humanity as a whole has no single and central consciousness. To be sure, we speak by accommodation of the social consciousness, the spirit of the age, the *Zeitgeist*, the national will; we speak of nations, associations, corporations, churches, and humanity itself, as persons; we apply personal pronouns to social wholes. But we mean those purposes which numerous individuals have in common, and through which they are able to coöperate. The figure of an organism is, however, a very apt figure to express the variety and coördination of many persons in society. Society is regarded as almost identical in all respects with a true organism, just because there is so much of unity in variety. Society that is worthy of the name can exist only in the coöperation of variously endowed individuals in the economic, the political, the moral, the purely social, and the religious spheres, and in the coördination of those great interests one with another.

Coördinated variety appears not only in the large but in the small. In any community or circle, variety is the law, the life, and the bond of society. Polite society, while certain conventionalities of dress and manner are observed alike by all, brings together persons of diverse gifts. The bond of union and interest is the contribution each makes to the common enjoyment. One is overflowing with information, another flashes with brilliancy of repartee, another is a clever *raconteur*, another supplies musical skill. What agreeable society in this place! it is said. It is agreeable because, with no clashing, there are so many kinds of talents and gifts.[1] But there is no thought of inequality. No one attempts to decide or thinks of deciding whether musical skill is equal to wit or not. There is no standard of comparison. Both are enjoyed. Both are components of the pleasure which depends on variety of contribution. Musicians may receive pecuniary compensation, while wits are not yet paid for dining out. But the value of talents is not measured by money. On the larger scale of civilization the functions of individuals are various and are related, but equality and inequality need not be emphasized. The painting of a pic-

[1] *Moral Evolution*, p. 31.

ture is not equal (nor unequal) to the invention of a telephone transmitter. The authorship of a book is not equal (nor unequal) to the leadership of an orchestra. Successful banking is not equal (nor unequal) to successful preaching. Statesmanship is not equal (nor unequal) to generalship. The work of a farmer is not equal (nor unequal) to the work of an engineer. These are various functions, all indispensable in the one great body of many members.

Neither are individuals exhaustively inventoried by their specific functions and contributions. Production may be single and reception various. One may receive and enjoy more or less than another of that which is supplied by the various functions of many producers. One may have more or less capacity than another for æsthetic or intellectual appreciation, and in that sense the two may be regarded as unequal. But, at any rate, the several functions which are exercised, and the different kinds and degrees of receptiveness, connote the indispensable variety of civilization.

X

PROGRESS PRODUCES VARIETY

THE progress of society coincides with increasing variety of functions and tastes. In the next section progress will be definitely characterized. Here it is employed in the usual and general signification of advancing civilization.

The coincidence of variety with progress may be observed under two methods. One method is by the actual contrast of advanced with rudimentary societies. Savagery is uniformity. The principal distinctions are sex, age, size, and strength. Savages divide up the work a little. They think alike or not at all, and converse therefore in monosyllables. There is scarcely any variety, only a horde of men, women, and children. The next higher stage, which is called barbarism, is marked by increased variety of functions. There is some division of labor, some interchange of thought, better leadership, more intellectual and æsthetic cultivation. The highest stage, which is called civilization, shows the greatest degree of specialization. Distinct functions become more numerous. Mechanical, commercial, educational, scientific, political, and artistic occupations multiply. The rudimentary societies are characterized by the likeness of equality; the developed societies are marked by the unlikeness of inequality or variety. As we go down, monotony; as we go up, variety. As we go down, persons are more alike; as we go up, persons are more unlike. It certainly seems, on the surface, as though approach to equality is decline towards the conditions of savagery, and as though variety is an advance towards higher civilization.

The other method by which the coincidence of variety with progress may be observed is an application, at least by way of analogy, of the law of evolution to social progress. The great apostle of evolution finds a law to which he thinks all development is obedient, the law of movement from homogeneity to heterogeneity and from heterogeneity to unity. Without turning aside to examine the entire meaning and the limitations of this law, we recognize its truth for the advance from savagery to civilization. The discoveries, inventions, arts, and philosophies of men appear in a certain independence of one another, almost sporadically. Fire, iron, utensils, ornaments, navigation hugging the shore or driven out of sight of land, astronomy applied to navigation, spears and shields instead of clubs and stones, black ships of the Achaians and fortified walls of Troy, gunpowder, dynamite, electricity, printing, a thousand appliances of construction and destruction are stumbled upon. Life is stirring. Dead uniformity is broken up. Homogeneity gives way to heterogeneity. The heterogeneous acquisitions, pursuits, and ambitions come into collision. Conflict and struggle ensue. Quarrels break out between the herdsmen of Lot and of Abraham, between the Hebrew slave and the Egyptian taskmaster, between baron and serf, between king and baron, between the nobility and commoners, between Protestant and Catholic, between Cavalier and Roundhead, between workmen and masters, between tradition and science, between science and religion. Homogeneity produces no variety and no conflict. Heterogeneity is collision on the way to adjustment. The old fighting areas become the settled country of coöperation and unity. On the frontier the elements of developing heterogeneity are in contention. But contestants become allies. Each receives from the other. Conquerors adopt the arts and laws of the conquered. It has been sagaciously observed that after the conflict of science and religion, science is more spiritual and religion is more rational.[1] They are as different as ever,

[1] President W. J. Tucker in a recent course of lectures at Andover Theological Seminary.

as different as light and heat, but have the same source in the divine wisdom, power, and love, as light and heat have the same solar source. The antagonism of heterogeneity has given place to the coördination of higher unity. But the new unity is not the old homogeneity. That was uniformity; this is unity. Savagery and civilization are the same human family dwelling on the same old mother earth. But the wilderness has become a cultivated field, and the nomad tribe has become the modern State.

Mr. Mallock makes the acute observation that in savagery there is coördination, in civilization subordination; that is, that, while savages are not so many individuals working with entire independence of one another, each supplying all his own wants, while there is some exchange of products, there is no subdivision of labor, but only a division. Some savages hunt, some fish, some build huts, some make rude clothing, yet all the processes of each industry are performed by the individual who engages in it, — a rude coördination; but in civilization each art is organized, each industry is in many parts by subdivision and subordination of the less to the greater, the parts to the whole. Savage coördination is equality. Civilized subordination is the inequality (if one chooses to call it that) of multiplied variety.

When it was believed that the village community was the primitive society of England and Germany and that slavery and serfdom followed as a retrogression which survives in tenancy and wages, some reformers pictured that primitive state as the ideal state to which we should return. There was, so the theory ran, common ownership of land occupied by freemen, with collective tillage, production, and distribution. It seems now to be established that the large section of land occupied and tilled by a community in coöperation was owned in every case by some powerful individual, the overlord, who exacted half or more of the entire labor on his own land which was interspersed in strips or was adjacent, or both, afterwards exacted half or more of the produce, later took money payments in the shape of annual rents, and finally, to some extent, gave life and hereditary leases, which amount to practical though limited ownership; that the movement was from slavery and serfdom (the original condition) to tenancy and possession, that every step was a step forwards, not only in improved agriculture, but also in the betterment of the people in comfort and intelligence. Even if those early communities were self-governing owners of the soil, working and sharing equally, they were but barely removed from starvation; there was no incentive to improved methods; they repeated the old two-field and three-field cultivation, and pursued the narrow circle of seedtime and harvest in almost entire ignorance of other communities. As soon as some individualism was permitted, as soon as a farmer could have his strips together instead of scattered, as soon as he could have the same section year after year instead of annual removal to other sections, as soon as his time was his own and he could pay rent, as soon as a life or hereditary lease made him a private proprietor, he and the whole community made progress. Agriculture was specialized and the several products exchanged; some men spent all their time weaving, shoemaking, building; towns and cities grew; schools and universities arose; in a word, there was that variety of agricultural, mechanical, commercial, and intellectual pursuits which constitutes civilization and marks the path of progress.

The only common ownership lay back of those early communities of serfs who were under a lord. It was the tribal system which survived for a long time in Wales and elsewhere. But that was merely the nomadic life of a few hundred men who roamed over an unoccupied territory, whose huts were set up on the shore near good fishing ground and abandoned at any time for other locations, who did not practice agriculture to any great extent, and who occasionally huddled together under chiefs to fight for the protection of their territory from invasion.

All signs, then, point in one direction. Equality is retrogression towards the dead uniformity and precarious life of stupid savagery, of nomadic tribes, and of serfdom. Progress is marked by private ownership, by specializing of pursuits, by organization, by unity in variety.

Equality of individuals would make society a windmill with so many similar arms which merely turn around and around as the wind may chance to blow, and is forever stationary. At the most, it performs simple and irregular work. Variety of individuals makes society a noble ship, with sails of different shape and size, with nice adjustment of ropes and pullies, with intelligence at the helm, — a structure which takes advantage of every wind and makes constant progress. I was amused to find, after I had hit upon this comparison, that Mr. Bellamy has chosen the windmill as the symbol of his new society. From the air-ship in which his two chief personages floated over Boston, the dome of the State House was noticed, and upon it a huge windmill was perceived. "What on earth have you stuck up there? . . . Surely that is an odd sort of ornament for a public building." "It is not intended as an ornament, but a symbol," replied the doctor. "It represents the modern ideal of a proper system of government. The mill stands for the machinery of administration, the wind that drives it symbolizes the public will, and the rudder that always keeps the vane of the mill before the wind, however suddenly or completely the wind may change, stands for the method by which the administration is kept at all times responsive and obedient to the mandate of the people, though it be but a breath." As they floated over the harbor scarcely a ship was to be seen. Commerce had ceased because each nation provided for all its own wants. With the passing away of the ship and the enthronement of the windmill, we may be well content to let the Socialism of vacillating equilibrium revolve aimlessly, and may let those who have no more serious business run a tilt against it in company with Don Quixote and his squire.

NOTE. — On page 78 certain theories of the early village communities of England are mentioned. A new theory is advocated in a book recently published by Professor Maitland of the University of Cambridge. He thinks the early settlers were freemen, but that there was no common ownership. According to this theory the primitive state was private ownership, and the only communism was joint cultivation by serfs at a later period. There is no comfort for socialists in that theory. In any case, the primitive state was, as I said, but barely removed from starvation, and progress followed the lines indicated.

XI

PROGRESS AND WANTS

IN the preceding section the promise was made that progress would be more definitely characterized in this section. That promise should not awaken the hope that progress will be described and defined exhaustively; for, even if that were possible, a volume instead of a short section would be required. In one essential respect, however, progress can be characterized definitely, and in that respect it is closely related to the variety and corresponding inequalities of men. Those conditions which are seen to be advance rather than stagnation, onward movement rather than repetition and retrogression, have one unfailing mark or note.

Progress is increase of legitimate wants which can be satisfied. The repeated satisfaction of old wants may be a good condition, but is not progress. The individual makes progress by the addition of an enjoyment, a knowledge, a possession. He makes a discovery, adds an accomplishment, cultivates a taste, makes a friend. If he merely rotates in a routine of repetition he may have many satisfactions, as one enjoys three meals every day and eight hours' sleep every night, but he is not making progress. Society advances by the consciousness and supply of new wants, from improved methods of locomotion and communication to widening knowledge of nature and history, to more beautiful products of art, to finer culture, to purer morality, and to more spiritual religion.

It is characteristic of man that the supply of one want awakens another want, and that thus he makes progress; and also, since he is not in isolation, but feels wants in company with and dependence on his fellows, that thus society makes progress. I take pleasure in quoting from a discerning writer a statement which can hardly be improved: "Except the satisfaction of one want plants at the same time the germ of another, there is an end of progress in any given direction. Wants, therefore, the most mysterious outcome of the process, are at the same time its motive power. There is no intelligent evolution without them. They are the rungs of the ladder by which we mount. Whence they come we know not. Why, when one want is satisfied, another higher up in the scale should take its place, we cannot begin to conceive. Rational creatures though we be, these unforeseen increments of evolution never cease to surprise us.

Every time a new want makes its appearance we awake to the fact that we are *new creatures*. It seemed, as we looked forward, as if the requirements of life would be met by the satisfaction of wants of which we were then conscious. But now, while the old creature is satisfied, the new one has all the restlessness and importunity of youth. This is the pledge to us of the possibility of further evolution and of attendant happiness. The true line of progressive being, therefore, is clearly indicated to be that in which there will be no cessation of wants that may be progressively realized." [1]

Progress, then, consists in the increase of wants, or, which is the same thing, in the development of men in the consciousness and satisfaction of capacities and tastes.

There is apparently no limit to possible additions of intellectual, æsthetic, moral, and religious development in the satisfaction of corresponding wants. The oldest and, in some respects, the most convincing argument for immortality is the inadequacy of the present life for possible attainments and enjoyments. A lifetime is too short for the mastery of a single science; yet, so far as capacity goes, given time enough, a scholar might master all the sciences. A thousand years would be none too long for an intellectual man to attain the know-

[1] *What is Reality?* by Francis Howe Johnson, p. 505.

ledge of science, history, philosophy, fine arts, literature, languages, and religions, which is now attained in separate portions by many men. One must be content, just for want of time, to leave vast regions of knowledge unexplored, although one is conscious of capabilities which would enable him to traverse them intelligently. So the scholar marks out his one line and follows it, nor presumes to boast that all knowledge is his province. Only a beginning has been made in those moral discernments, obligations, and reciprocities which will make the perfectly good man in the perfectly good society. To a future century the moralities of to-day may seem as crude as the rude bravery, the bristling honor, and the coarse customs of " Merrie England " seem to us. For communities, nations, society at large, no limit is defined beyond which progress in the awakening and supply of wants cannot go. Sounder economics, wiser and purer politics, more equitable jurisprudence, finer æsthetics, better ethics, more humane and spiritual religion are easily imagined and confidently expected. Progress of the individual and of society, which is individuals in relations, consists of accretions of knowledge, justice, beauty, and goodness, which are gained by degrees as the desires for them strengthen into felt and imperative wants. There is no known limit to the development of men in the awakening and satisfaction of various wants, and therefore no limit to the advance of society in the progressive realization of wants. Without lingering to discriminate between wants the satisfaction of which promotes well-being and fancied wants the satisfaction of which is injurious, and without lingering to observe that different individuals have different wants, I proceed at once to consider the relation of progress through the satisfaction of legitimate wants to the inequality and variety of individuals.

XII

VARIETY PRODUCES PROGRESS

COMPARISON of developed with rudimentary societies has shown that progress results in variety of functions. It now appears, in view of the relation of progress to wants, that variety of functions is a necessary condition of progress. The differentiation of individuals, which is indicated in their various capacities and pursuits, is a cause quite as much as a result. It both constitutes and produces progress.

If wants are to be satisfied, supply must correspond to demand. If wants are numerous, sources of supply must be various. Existing wants, for which provision is constantly made in large measure, are satisfied by the contributions of many dissimilar producers. Provision for one person for a single day is made by numerous toilers. The food and clothing one needs are supplied from all parts of the world by manifold kinds of labor and skill. Transportation from place to place is provided by an army of inventors, constructors of vehicles, engine-drivers, and motor-men. The newspapers and books one reads, the music one enjoys, the pictures one admires, the plays one witnesses, supply wants by the productiveness of many hand and brain workers. One adds his daily mite to the common store, and draws out in return the comforts and enjoyments of his own life. Should no more be done than to maintain present conditions, should men have only the advantages of existing civilization, a great variety of unlike and unequal functions must be exercised. Certainly, then, if progress is to be made by added satisfactions, there must be even more variety of functions, new and finer differentiations of training and pursuits. Every step of progress means the addition of a human factor that is in some way unlike all existing factors. The progress of civilization, then, cannot be a nearer approach to equality, but must be an increasing diversification of the individuals that compose society, a more complicated and not a more simple organism. There must be articulation of each new invention and art, of fresh knowledge, and of broader application of moral principles with the organisms into which they are introduced. The new factors multiply the power of those factors which are already active, as a little cog inserted at the right place in a mechanism doubles the revolutions and the transmitted powers of all the wheels.

Beyond the most meagre margin, the individual cannot supply his own wants, but, as he advances, is more and more dependent on others. He who does all for himself leads a starved and empty life. When as consumer an individual is the only customer of himself as producer; when he engages in no traffic with another as buyer or seller, if such a condition were possible, he is a man reduced to the lowest terms, not so much of a man as a savage in a tribe; he is a wild man of the woods.

All this is commonplace which may seem to be hardly worth stating. Of course we all are dependent on one another, and become more and more dependent as wants increase, as life is more rich and various, as anything worthy the name of progress is achieved. But these trite facts play havoc with theories of equality. They emphasize the growing variety and difference of persons. They show that the nearer man and society approach the ideal state, the more unlike do individuals become; that even if all have the same amount of money in their pockets, they will use their money in ways as different as wants, desires, tastes, and capacities are different, if for no other reason just because wants, which are many and various, must be supplied by individuals who are unlike in skill and capacity.

XIII

SUPERIORITY

THE word "superiority" which was laid aside lest it should seem invidious may now be employed without offense. Every one who contributes to the supply of legitimate and increasing wants is, in respect to his contribution, superior to others, at least in the sense that others are dependent on him. Those who satisfy, for themselves and for others, the higher wants, may be regarded as superior to those who satisfy only the lower wants. Above the plane of material wants (although variety of function is necessary even to material production) are intellectual, political, and æsthetic wants, for the satisfaction of which there must be some persons who are superior to others. A youth desires education. He must put himself under teachers who are his superiors, or at least must have recourse to books written by those who have already attained the knowledge he wishes to acquire. Directly or indirectly wisdom is received from other minds. Is a man, exactly like me, who knows no more than I know, to make provision for my intellectual wants? There is no such thing as a self-taught man, as there is no such thing as a self-made man. When a purse-proud merchant said to a would-be son-in-law, "I am a self-made man, sir," there was justice in the reply, "You are under no obligation to confess to me." One who desires to be a pianist looks for a teacher who excels in technique, touch, and interpretation, or has at least been a pupil of some great master. Superiority is insisted upon. That there may be learners there must be teachers in advance of the students. The proficiency and talent of a few is the necessary condition of the progress of the many.

But who teaches the teachers? They teach one another. The teacher himself, not being omniscient, learns from those who have the knowledge he does not possess. The philosopher must know something of science. But a lifetime is required for the mastery of a single science. The philosopher, who relates facts to principles, must be content to take results which specialists have obtained. Scientifically they are his superiors. He regards them as authorities before whom he bows, as they, in turn, should bow before him as an authority in his own province, although scientists have attempted, to their confusion, to be their own philosophers oftener than philosophers have tried to be their own scientists. The biologist teaches the geologist, they teach the philosopher and are taught by him, and the poet teaches them all. Each, in some particular, is superior to the others, and each discovering, in his own line of research, new facts and truths, stands, for a time, the superior of all, a purveyor to a new want which his discovery supplies.

This is just as true in politics. Laws are not self-evident to all men. Government is not automatic. There must be those who understand the structure and needs of society, who have knowledge of political principles, who know what interests should be left to individuals, and what provinces of action should be regulated by law, and to whom authority is delegated for the enactment and execution of laws. It will not be claimed that all citizens are equally well fitted to legislate for the million. There are enough fit men in the United States to govern the nation aright. If the right men were in the right places welfare and progress would be promoted. The mischief is that superior knowledge and fitness are not recognized and enthroned.

The interests of economics furnish no exception to the dependence of progress on superiority. There must be organization and therefore organizers. There must be workmen under direction.

Development of productiveness, increase of wealth, and proper distribution of goods are possible as superior persons invent and control. Such persons cannot be drawn by lot nor chosen before trial. They must be created under strong incentives and competitions, which are the conditions of selection for important functions. Economic evils are due to the control of incompetent and unprincipled men and to the misplacement of competent men in subordinate positions; to grants of artificial monopoly and to corrupt legislation, rather than to a system which offers rewards in the shape of well-earned profits, or to unequal sharing of material values.

The socialist colony of Ruskin, in Tennessee, has a number of by-laws, one of which is: "Every member of this Association shall surrender his natural freedom which leads him to disregard the rights of others, for the sake of civil or social freedom, which, being based upon the principles of justice, has regard for his rights and for the rights of all." The question at once arises, To whom is natural freedom surrendered? Evidently to certain persons who are supposed to be better capable than others of managing the affairs of the colony. Therefore another by-law provides that "all orders of foremen and superintendents must at all times be obeyed." This is the only possible condition of successful business, although, if individual freedom is relinquished, it may easily be perverted to tyranny.

I have said that every productive person is in some respects superior to others. It may now be observed that two conditions are necessary to progress: one, that each make the most and the best of himself, a condition in which he is dependent on his many superiors; the other, that each render the service of which he is capable in promoting the welfare, the knowledge, or the enjoyment of others, a condition, in respect to such service rendered, in which he is their superior. Then there can be progress all along the line, each person communicating a pull which is felt at all points and by all persons.

XIV

ARISTOCRACY AND DEMOCRACY

At the top and in the lead should be the real aristocracy. That good word has suffered a perversion which has nearly destroyed its signification. Aristocracy means the rule of the best. If the best men have guidance and control, progress is constantly made. If the real aristocracy is set aside in favor of the incompetent, there is confusion and every evil work. Honor to the Greeks, who coined the word that stands for the rule of the best. When the word is corrupted so that it signifies pride of rank, or birth, or wealth, with compulsion of menial service from others, with indolence and luxuriousness, both parts of the word lose their original meaning. The first part no longer means the best, but comes to mean the worst; the latter part no longer means ruling, but means exaction of homage. But there are those who are fitted to be a political, an economic, an intellectual aristocracy. Place them in their useful and rightful positions, let the aristocracy of merit be enthroned as well as acknowledged, and

there will be that government, that national welfare, and that culture which constitute well-being
and insure progress. A great overturning there
might be, indeed. Some who are first would be
last, and some who are last would be first. Some
who are exalted would be abased, and some who
are abased would be exalted. But there would
still be a few first, a few last, and a multitude at
all points between. The ideal society would, no
doubt, reverse many positions of the actual society.
We are told in the Talmud of a young Jew who
had quitted the sphere of earth, but was permitted
to return to it and give his impressions of heaven
and hell. "What hast thou seen in the other
world, my son?" asked the Rabbi Levi, his father.
"I have seen an inverted world; they who here
were highly exalted were abased in the depths;
they who are last here take there the highest place."
"It is the true world thou hast seen, my son," said
the elder Rabbi.[1] But even in the ideal state there
is no dead level of equality.

Francis Galton[2] classified Englishmen according
to ability and reputation in seven grades, from A,
the lowest, to G, the highest. He found two hundred
and fifty thousand in a million in the lowest grade,
a decreasing proportion in each superior grade,

[1] *The Message of Israel*, by Julia Wedgwood.
[2] *Hereditary Genius*.

and only fourteen in the highest, with one left over, marked X, standing solitary and alone above G, carrying his flag high above the social pyramid. An accurate classification might have employed all the letters of the alphabet, or even have used a million numerals to designate the differences in a million people, but there would still be the few who by intellectual superiority and unbounded energy are the born leaders, teachers, judges, rulers, and benefactors, — the genuine aristocracy.

Otto Ammon[1] points out the striking fact that the idea of equality originated with the aristocracy. "The principle," he says, "of equality springs originally from the circle of the nobility, and was first applied to all men by the ideas of the French Revolution. But aristocratic equality is altogether different from democratic equality. The former limits itself downwards against the pressing in of inharmonious elements, and it has a deep thought; one shall be as much as another, *no one less.* Democratic equality limits itself upwards; one shall be as little as another, *no one more!* Whoever in spirit and character is superior shall be dragged down into the dust, so that his presence may not violate the principle." Neither of these notions is correct. The true principle is, to every

[1] *Die Gesellschaftsordnung und ihre Natürlichen Grundlagen,* pp. 194, 195.

man his work, his place, and his right, without
regard to less or more. But the vivid contrast of
ideas makes the two tendencies distinct and implies
the truth that there are superior functions, and
therefore must be superior men. It implies that,
if superior functions are in abeyance, or still worse,
if inferior men attempt to exercise functions of
leadership, progress will be arrested.

The French writer who has already been cited
applies to the true leaders and teachers, upon
whom national and racial progress chiefly depends,
a word signifying well-born, the word *eugéniques*.
He applies it to those who are superior by reason
of ability, energy, and character. By well-born he
does not mean an hereditary nobility and gentry,
but those whose ancestry combines the best physical and intellectual qualities. He maintains that
in the golden age of Greece the really great men
bore rule in politics, philosophy, and art. He believes that the vitality, enterprise, and expansion
of the Anglo-Saxons is due to fortunate strains of
blood and the leadership of the true *eugéniques*.
He contends that the decadence of the French is to
be attributed to inferior racial mixture and to the
promotion of inferior men to positions of power.
He finds scientific evidence of his opinion in cra-
nial measurements, the long-headed peoples being
progressive and the short-headed peoples being

decadent. I cannot go with Lapouge to all his conclusions. But he stands on important facts. I am willing to go with him the mile, although he shall not compel me to go with him twain. The fact that progress depends on the rule, or at least on the influence and service of those who by inheritance and development are endowed with superior gifts, is a fact which should be gladly acknowledged.

Returning to Ammon, I agree with him that the chief hindrances to progress are unfitness, misplacement, and maladjustment. He points out several conditions of that sort which are detrimental. He regards it as detrimental when gifted men are obliged to employ themselves in subordinate positions and are hindered from passing to their appropriate places; when incompetent and senescent persons are retained in responsible offices; when talented but ill-balanced and prejudiced men are set to administer justice; when the leading class have excessive power and legislate in their own interest, or the centre of gravity is shifted to the under classes which lack the insight requisite to right decisions, or the whole social interest is directed, even if sympathetically, upon the proletariat; when the household economy of the higher classes presses so hard that anxiety about daily bread prevents free service to the community;

when the independent position of the middle class is lost; when skilled workmen have no assured employment; when, in the education of youth, school organization subjects all pupils to the old-fashioned classical training and does not educate in accordance with their personal bent for mercantile, industrial, and scientific pursuits; and, in general, when competition is hindered and the development of energy is arrested.[1]   If the worst men and the least capable come into control, on the assumption that one man is as good as another, the aristocracy of merit is replaced by a misrule which deserves the ill-meaning and ill-sounding designation, kakistocracy, the rule of the worst.

The task of democracy is practically achieved when it invariably selects the aristocracy of merit and capacity for the highest functions, and matches position to fitness all the way up and down the line.   This, indeed, is the fundamental principle of democracy, not to make all men equal, but to recognize superiority and to place power in the hands of the wisest and most capable men, always to put the right man in the right place and to consign the hustling demagogue to the privacy of well-earned obscurity.   Democracy should replace the aristocracy which depends on accident of birth by the aristocracy of merit, should set aside the

[1] *Die Gesellschaftsordnung*, pp. 189–192.

aristocracy which buys place with gold for that which earns place by capability and distinguished service. But when democracy stands for a great leveling down and a slight leveling up, when it will have no aristocracy at all, its doom is sealed.

That the task of democracy is recognition of the true aristocracy, municipal and national problems plainly show. When closely packed populations unite under one government to become the chief metropolis of a State and, indeed, of the nation, it is seen that the prosperity and the political health of the municipality depend almost entirely on electing to the magistracy the most capable, intelligent, and honest citizen, and on electing as heads of departments those citizens who are best fitted by success in business and public affairs to conduct those departments. It is seen that the worst calamity is promotion of dishonest and incapable men to a control so responsible. The laws of the charter may be ever so good, but will be inefficient in the hands of bad or inferior men. The laws may be imperfect, and yet if they are enforced by suitable men, the city will be well governed.

The jubilee which celebrates the sixtieth anniversary of the coronation of Queen Victoria has been the occasion of many inquiries into the reasons of the wonderful expansion of Great Britain during her long reign, an expansion unequaled by any nation in any period of history. One writer, after making allowance for the improved mechanisms of the century, — steam, electricity, railroads, telegraphs, telephones, all that multiplication of forces which enables one man to do the work of a hundred men, which makes what were formerly the luxuries of the rich the necessaries and conveniences of all, but which are the common possession of all the civilized nations ; and after making allowance for the freedom which has struck off many shackles from trade and given political rights to all, and which was long regarded as a panacea for all evils, — calls attention to another cause without which freedom would be a fiction, a cause which has given England her superiority over other nations for the last half century.

"But freedom is not all. There is something else in the progress of England in this century of which we are conscious, something that we do not perhaps always like to acknowledge, but which, notwithstanding our own millions and our own wealth, we may well envy her. There is no word for it in the dictionaries, it is not celebrated on tombstones or in biographies, but it is a quality without which no nation or individual has ever made any stable progress in the history of the world — perhaps we should say an assemblage of qualities which may be more easily traced in the effects they produce than named. In this century for the first time a great power, comparable at its height only to that of Rome, has come upon the scene, which has known how, in every department of government, to select the best man for the work. The English judge, the English parliamentary leader and minister, the English consul, ambassador, civil servant, and military and naval officer, form a body of public men such as hardly any other country possesses, and certainly such as England never possessed before. Not merely is there no corruption among them, but they form a natural *classe dirigeante* — they are as nearly as may be the picked men of the country. In other words, the English public service draws to itself the character and intelligence of the whole country, and those who govern are in a larger measure than anywhere else in the world those who ought to govern."

The writer adds that " for this scheme of government it was necessary, not, as was supposed in the last century, that we should have a new heaven and a new earth, but that the notion of privilege should be replaced by that of a trust, and that improvement should be sought through the enlightened discharge of duty and not through aggression. The example of England shows that hereafter this view of government is the only one for those who do not wish to fall back into the night of despotism and decay. Whenever England has followed this path, prosperity and power have attended her; whenever she has relapsed into the old system, as has been more than once the case in foreign affairs, the result has been disaster and humiliation."[1] This, in some respects, is a rose-colored view, pardonable in the year of jubilee. England is not without English (and Irish) critics, as witness Lecky's "Democracy." Such criticism is a healthy and hopeful sign. But the writer quoted has undoubtedly hit upon the cause of the expansion and prosperity of England in this century. It is democracy placing the reins in the hands of its real aristocracy.

Mr. Godkin, writing on the "Decline of Legislatures," finds the reason for the decline in the inferiority of the members. He says: "It is increasingly difficult to get a man of serious knowledge on any subject to go to Congress if he have other pursuits and other sources of income. To get him to go to the State legislature, in any of the populous and busy States, is well-nigh impossible." When Congress adjourns, and when the legislature adjourns, a sense of relief pervades the community. Mr. Godkin contrasts legislatures with Constitutional Conventions, which command the highest respect, and shows that the chief difference is in the supe-

[1] *The Nation*, June 24, 1897.

rior ability and character of the members of Conventions. His own language should be given : —

" Side by side with the annual or biennial legislature we have another kind of legislature, the ' Constitutional Convention,' which retains everybody's respect, and whose work, generally marked by care and forethought, compares creditably with the legislation of any similar body in the world. Through the hundred years of national existence it has received little but favorable criticism from any quarter. It is still an honor to have a seat in it. The best men in the community are still eager or willing to serve in it, no matter at what cost to health or private affairs. I cannot recall one convention which has incurred either odium or contempt. Time and social changes have often frustrated its expectations, or have shown its provisions for the public welfare to be inadequate or mistaken, but it is very rare indeed to hear its wisdom and integrity questioned. In looking over the list of those who have figured in the conventions of the State of New York since the Revolution, one finds the name of nearly every man of weight and prominence ; and few lay it down without thinking how happy we should be if we could secure such service for our ordinary legislative bodies." [1]

[1] "The Decline of Legislatures," by E. L. Godkin, D. C. L.: *The Atlantic Monthly*, July, 1897.

A wise man said of the Christian society: "God hath set some in the Church; first apostles, secondly prophets, thirdly teachers, then gifts of healing, helps, governments, divers kinds of tongues." The divine order in the Church is the order of nature in all progressive human societies. By endowment and by corresponding increment of training God hath set some in society: first poets, preachers, and philosophers; secondly statesmen and legislators; thirdly teachers, scientists, and inventors; then merchants, manufacturers, navigators, military commanders, mechanics, farmers, spinners, miners, clerks, cooks, butlers, tailors, athletes. Are all philosophers? are all statesmen? are all inventors? are all mechanics? are all weavers, cooks, or tailors? But the poet cannot say to the farmer, I have no need of thee; nor yet the weaver to the statesman, I have no need of thee. The same wise man said that, in the harmony of mutual regard and service, persons are not exhaustively defined by nationality, status, and sex; there is neither Greek nor Jew, there is neither bond nor free, there is neither male nor female, but all are one (not equal) in Christ Jesus, in the life of mutual dependence, and in the spirit of love. One wiser than Paul said that the measure of greatness is the measure of service to others; "whosoever will be great among you, let him be your minister, and whosoever will be chief among you, let him be your servant." That is the true social law, applying not only to superior gifts and powers, but to all talent, skill, knowledge, and character; the measure of power the measure of service. Since the service must be various, the gifts and powers must be various.

When nature is allowed to determine function, artificial arrangements are broken up, and the first places are accorded to those who are entitled to them. The seat of honor may be placed here or placed there; but where McGregor is, there is the head of the table. I was once asked which is the best and most desirable chair in a theological institution, and could only answer, the chair which is occupied by the best man.

Misplacements are not without their consolations to observers. A great office does not make its occupant great. A fool, thrust into prominence by holding a high office, only shows more conspicuously how great a fool he is. A life-size statue surmounting a dome is dwindled into pygmy insignificance. When the man and the office are in inverse proportion, the sober judgment of the people perceives and deplores the maladjustment. Official promotion may fall to unworthy men, but they do not escape a just estimate of their unfitness. It is pretty well known when a man is too small for his place. It is not pleasant, I should think, to perceive surprise on all sides when one is appointed to an important position or receives an honorary degree. Surprise because one is not promoted and honored would be more agreeable. After all, then, promotion is not real unless it is deserved, and is valued almost precisely according to the worth and ability of the man himself. A popular ovation having been given to an unpopular President, a local newspaper significantly observed that the people honor the office. Correct estimate of unfitness is a sure indication that the people wish to enthrone the aristocracy of fitness, and that in the end they will succeed.

Professor Paulsen, tracing the educational ideal of the future, says that " the society corresponding to the above ideal would be that of an aristocracy of mind. Is this the type towards which we are leaning? Is the aristocracy of birth and wealth to be supplanted by the aristocracy of personal worth and merit? This has been the philosopher's dream from the day of Plato's Republic to the present hour. It is the tendency of nature. It would be the aristocracy of nature to have every individual stand independently upon his own personal merit, and not upon the achievements of his father; while the influence of heredity, in the sense of the transmission of personal characteristics, would certainly not be diminished. Such is the aristocracy to which historical development seems to point. Both Church and State have made considerable advances toward the realization of this idea of a personal *élite*, by bestowing position and influence according to the degree of personal talent and efficiency without regard to birth and possession." [1]

It follows, with many other conclusions, that those who are capable of great service should not shun it from fear of criticism or of lack of appreciation, nor because high office has been degraded by unworthy occupants. We may sympathize with but cannot applaud the choice of Ulysses to be a private citizen, the lot he would have taken if he had had the first instead of the last choice.

[1] *The Forum*, August, 1897.

XV

RESENTMENT OF SUPERIORITY AND INFERIORITY

RESENTMENT of superiority is a characteristic mark of prevalent discontent. It is a discouraging symptom and a hindrance to progress. Resentment of undeserved fortune has some justification. Over-estimation, stamped by conferring honors on men who are conspicuous only by some happy accident, deserves criticism. But when resentment is excited by deserved wealth and by real superiority, it actually prevents the full measure of social service which the wealthy and gifted can render. A gentleman provokes the dislike of a boor just because he is a gentleman. The boor goes out of his way to be rude in order to assert his equality, and chuckles to himself as he makes a coarse and profane reply to a civil question. He does not know how to handle the gentleman, and in the end is defeated, only to resent refinement all the more. Ignorant voters will not tolerate the scholar and the gentleman in politics. They call for an " every-day man " who is " one of the people." On the platform a candidate is tempted to condescend to vulgarity and profanity in order to catch votes. Politicians from some sections of the country offend the social proprieties by appearing at evening receptions in other than evening garments, for fear of offending their constituents by dressing as gentlemen. He who confers benefits must be careful not to assume a tone or manner of superiority. Benefactors have to be wary. On their part there may be no pride in their capability of service, no feeling of patronage or condescension, and yet they cannot go directly towards the fulfillment of their benevolent designs, but must proceed by indirection, almost by stealth, when they would bestow charity, convey information, or proffer counsel. The benefactor must not only keep his left hand in ignorance of his right hand's helpfulness to guard against the pride of goodness, but must keep his helpful right hand itself out of the sight of the beneficiary, lest it be bitten by the ingratitude of resentful envy. This resentment of superiority is one of the voices that clamor for equality, but it has no other idea of equality than leveling all superiority down to its own inferiority.

There is also resentment of inferiority on the part of the superior, which, although not as ignoble as the other sort, may be even more unfavorable to the common welfare. The cry for equality is in the mouths of some who, with the best motives (let us be charitable), desire to remove the limitations of nature from those who are less amply endowed than others, to carry on a " reform against nature."   Early missionaries to savage tribes were stirred by resentment of the natural as well as of the moral inferiority of savages, and attempted to convert them, not only from cruelty to kindness, but also from a rude social state to the refinements of European civilization, to equalize them with those who had had the advantage of generations of education and culture, and were the product of the finest racial and national stock.   Professor F. Ratzel, in his " History of Mankind," referring to a missionary in Terra del Fuego who was instructed to teach the natives agriculture, building, and other arts first, and who accomplished little, asks why the results were so meagre, and replies : " Such an attempt to bring men over from a poor but easy state of existence to one which, though better, demands more of them, can be nothing but an economic revolution which is not only capable of bringing blessings, but also certain to cause mischief, and the latter sooner than the former."

Some social reformers who cherish dreams of equality resent the condition of those who have little but physical strength and skill by which they can contribute to the supply of common wants.

Such friends, from whom they might pray to be saved, would give them a portion of goods which they would use harmfully, an education of which they are utterly incapable, and refinements which they can assume about as easily as a pine table can take a mahogany polish. As well attempt to impose upon savages the dress, manners, appliances, culture, and art of a ripe civilization as attempt by division of wealth, or by any economic redistribution, to put the refinements, cultivations, and enjoyments of the well-endowed into the possession of small endowment and attainment. These reformers impart their own resentment to those for whom it is felt by pointing out the contrast between employer and workman, between capital and labor, between the purple and fine linen of the wealthy and the homespun and calico of wage-earners, — always the material contrast, so easily perceived, but signifying so little for character, contentment, and enjoyment.

If we could get at the workers, if we could hear them speak for themselves, while those who profess to speak for them, but are not of them, keep silence for a little space, we might find that resentment of superiority is not so general as we had been led to suppose. There is much of it, no doubt, but it is, in so large part, instigated from without rather than incited from within that it is

safe to deduct a large discount from the estimate
of resentment made by professed reformers. In
the grades between the lowest and the highest
twentieths of the population (classified according
to material possessions), that is, in the grades of
employment which are above want and below
riches, it is doubtful if there would be much resentment of wealth and superiority, were it not
for agitators, themselves enjoying competence and
leisure, some of them possessing wealth, who
pursue the *dilettante* virtue of social reform, who
foment discontent by speeches and writings which
tell persons of moderate but sufficient income how
much better off some other people are than they
are ; were it not also for unscrupulous politicians
who hope to rally votes by inciting envy against
wealth, but who, between campaigns, are uncon-
cerned, or are rolling up for themselves the wealth
they have taught others to covet.   The minister of
a great congregation of German working-people in
New York city, after listening to an address before a clergyman's association on the discontent
of laborers who, it was alleged, would not long
endure existing inequality, quietly remarked that
it was not so with his people, that they were industrious, comfortable, and contented, and that only
three or four times in as many years had he heard
a word of complaint, or of envy towards the pro-

sperous. The case may be exceptional, but seems to be typical. This does not mean that working-people are without ambition and have no desire to better their circumstances, but it does signify that they are not continually brooding over the contrast of wealth and wages; that for the most part they go their ways contentedly, enjoying what they have, and cultivating the common virtues. Some reformers are, in fact, discouraged because many of the people actually do not have and will not be induced to have a proper resentment in view of the superior advantages of the prosperous who live at the other end of the avenue. But, whatever degree of resentment there may be and however it may be incited, it is beyond question that the resentment which would merely deprive others of what they have and would reduce superiority to a lower level is harmful chiefly to those who cherish it, and serves only to hinder such improvement as is possible.

XVI

TWO KINDS OF DISCONTENT

THERE are two kinds of discontent; a kind to be condemned and a kind to be encouraged: an ignoble and a noble discontent. The first has in view the material possessions and the superior endowments of others; the second has in view one's own possession, achievement, and character. The first is the discontent of envy; the other is the discontent of ambition.

The envy that is most common and most commonly appealed to is the envy excited by material values in the possession of others. It covets a neighbor's house, ox, and ass, and the means whereby he can afford to have a manservant and a maidservant. Envy of superior talents and of the eminence they give in literary, academic, and political circles is felt only by persons within those circles, by persons who are engaged in the pursuits in which a few have made a name for themselves. Those circles are small, and, within them, the majority are stimulated rather than embittered by the success of their superiors. For one unsuccessful or moderately successful author who is soured and who believes that the popularity of others is undeserved, there are a hundred authors who are genuine admirers and fair critics. But the masses do not so much as know the names of distinguished authors, scholars, scientists, and philosophers. Envy is most commonly excited by display of wealth. The envious imagine that the chief good consists in material values, that riches procure complete enjoyment, that money is the measure and the master of all things, that a good share of wealth is all that is necessary for attaining the objects of life. The discontent of ambition, on the other hand, desires the attainment, culture, and character which are dependent on one's own exertions.

The discontent of contrast deepens into bitterness as it sees that the envied wealth is out of reach. It despises that amount of wealth which is attainable by industry and thrift. It waits for a redistribution through which the poor will become richer by making the rich poorer. Those who nourish this discontent in others by emphasizing contrasts without appealing to personal ambition aggravate envy into hostility which only hinders more equitable adjustment. It is not from such discontent that progress comes. Unless other sentiments are fostered, the distance between extremes will be widened. Should the discontent of contrast become violence, the economic structure might, indeed, be overthrown, but only to involve all in ruin. Labor would be a blind Samson crushed itself in pulling down the house of the Philistines.

The discontent of ambition sees the better self, the better mechanic, better farmer, better husband and father, in existing conditions, sees that improved men make improved conditions, and sees that extremes can be reduced, not by pulling down the superior, but by raising the inferior in the measure of their capacity. Those who have a small share, perhaps too small a share of material goods, will get more, not by redivision of what there is, but by increased productiveness of skill. After a redistribution which gives equal shares to all, ignorance and laziness would soon be as destitute as ever. Even if wealth were parceled out equitably, it would not produce men of intelligence and character, or, at the most, would be only one factor among others for the improvement of men. For the making of character, the gaining of knowledge, and the right use of wealth, personal ambition and effort are necessary.

True ownership of wealth cannot be gained simply by taking it away from those who possess it. Material values, in that respect, are like mental and moral values. Intelligence cannot be gained by depriving the wise of part of their knowledge; nor refinement by robbing the cultivated of their culture; nor virtue by taking away the character of the good. Those values can be gained only by one's own ambition and toil. The gain of one is not the loss of another, but the gain of each is, or may be, the gain of many; as with religion, of which it has been said that the more we give away the more we have. Material goods change hands more easily than mental and moral goods are transferred, at least so far as legal title is concerned, but are not really possessed except as they are rightly used. Ownership is use. A man that is unfitted by ignorance, vanity, or selfishness for the right use of wealth· has no ownership in the goods that stand in his name. He may buy books enough to fill five hundred square feet of library shelves, but if he cannot read and appreciate them they are not his. Legal possession is not personal ownership. Money buys but a small part of intellectual and æsthetic value. Unless personal ambition incites to attainment and culture, wealth is no addition to resources. An intelligent workman reading a scientific treatise or a volume of history which he takes out of a public library becomes possessor of the value of the book, although it does not belong to him. A rich man who has no taste for reading does not possess his

private library, although he has paid for the costly
editions and has placed his name and imported
crest in every volume. An inquisitive boy asked
a driver as the horses toiled up the mountain road,
"Who owns Mount Washington?" The driver replied that it is owned by the Pingree heirs. But
the mountain really belongs to those who admire
its beauty and grandeur. Legal ownership has the
value only of so much timber.

Envy, seeing external possessions and coveting
them, is a foolish discontent which could make
only a meagre, selfish use of the wealth it would
grasp, and would add nothing to the sum total.
Ambition, using aright the goods already in hand,
increasing them by skill and industry, and aspiring after knowledge, culture, and character, makes
better men, who are fitted to use as much wealth
as they may obtain.

The same possessions, enjoyments, and culture
are not possible to all, because God has made
men unlike. But a degree of improvement is possible to every one. Let each seek that and not
grasp at the moon. The important thing is that
each know what he can do and what he can be,
and strive for that with all his might. Let the
rear come up, by all means, so that, if possible, it
may stand where the van is to-day. But let no one
suppose that the van will wait until all are ranged

along one line. The leaders will be as far in advance as ever. The rear moves up only because those in advance keep moving forward and in their movement lead or draw on those who are behind.

I am not preaching a gospel of satisfaction with economic conditions. Changes and improvements are needed and will probably occur. If legislation in the United States favors wealth and monopoly at the expense of toilers, it can be and should be reversed by the people. Yet, were economic conditions perfect, there would be no gospel of salvation, apart from the ambition and striving of the individual to become his best possible self in the use of that which he has. Nor are economic conditions so bad that right ambition need fail of realizing itself in those increments of intelligence and growths of character of which by endowment the individual is capable. There are, at any rate, voices enough crying in the wilderness to deepen the discontent of contrast. There cannot be too many voices calling individuals to turn from their ignorance and shiftlessness and to bring forth fruits worthy of repentance. To most men that are stirred by the ambition of discontent and are asking, What shall we do? the cry of the ancient voice is still a good answer: to publicans, representing the wealthy, " Extort no more than that which is appointed you;" to soldiers, representing the employed, "Extort from no man by violence, neither accuse any one wrongfully, and be content with your wages;" and to all classes, "Bring forth fruits worthy of repentance."

NOTE.—The statement on page 114 that the majority of workingmen are not envious of the wealthy may perhaps be questioned in view of the large number who are members of Trade Unions. But their object is simply to obtain fair wages, to receive the share to which they are fairly entitled. They understand perfectly that large capital in the hands of a few is the necessary condition of good wages.

XVII

ADMIRATION AND INSPIRATION

IN contrast with resentment of superiority is admiration. Admiration creates inspiration, arouses ambition, and promotes progress. Egotism and self-satisfaction make advancement impossible. The Master, as the pupils and friends of the late Professor Jowett of Oxford loved to call him, remarking that one of the two great forms of religion is the sense and practice of the presence of God, says: "The best of humanity is the most perfect reflection of God: humanity as it might be, not as it is; and the way up to Him is to be found in the lives of the best and greatest men; of saints and legislators and philosophers, the founders of states and the founders of religions, — allowing for and seeking to correct their necessary one-sidedness. These heroes, or demigods, or benefactors, as they would have been called by the ancients, are the mediators between God and man. Whither they went we also are going, and may be content to follow in their footsteps." This admiration, he adds, is prevented by overweening egotism. "We are always thinking of ourselves, hardly ever of God, or of great and good men who are His image. This egotism requires to be abated before we can have any real idea of His true nature. The 'I' is our God — What we shall eat? What we shall drink? What we shall do? How we shall have a flattering consciousness of our own importance?"[1]

Without great men how commonplace, and, it may well be believed, how unprogressive the world would be. Progress is possible for the individual who admires a superior. It may not be possible by other agencies, in the absence of a genuine admiration which inspires ambition. A college president, who, like the Master of Balliol, awakens enthusiasm for the highest standards, which he himself embodies, gives tone and uplift to the whole community of aspiring youth whom he governs and guides into self-guidance and self-government. The Governor of a State, who is a cultivated, capable, honest, and courageous gentleman, is the pride of the Commonwealth. He awakens an admiration and enthusiasm which raise the standard of citizenship and of official position, and which show that in their hearts the people prefer the refinement and greatness of one of nature's noblemen to the coarseness and meanness of the

[1] *Life and Letters of Benjamin Jowett*, vol. ii. p. 313.

politician who seeks to gain popularity by cheap arts.

Admiration of others is itself admirable. Some nobleness of spirit is needed to recognize nobleness. The saying that a man is not a hero to his valet has been wittily justified by the explanation that it is not because the hero is not a hero, but because the valet is a valet. Yet servants know the difference between noble and ignoble masters, and are said to be good judges of character. This may very well be true, for the reason that he who controls another reveals his character in the requirements he makes. The devotion and respect of servants are precious tributes paid to worth; and they also exalt those who are capable of such admiration and loyalty. Appreciation, which ennobles those who generously feel it, is found at all points up and down the social and intellectual scale. Darwin, so it is said, after receiving a visit from Gladstone, who was passing through Down, spoke of the visit afterwards, and declared that the great statesman sat and talked as familiarly as a neighbor, and that no one would have dreamed that he was Prime Minister of the kingdom. Appreciation of the greatness of the statesman made the scientist forget his own greatness. There is a fine touch in Stevenson's description of the old Scotchman on an emigrant ship who was filled with admiration of the indifferent performances of a youth on the fiddle, and who repeatedly called on the bystanders to share his enthusiasm.

The secret of modesty and of egotism is partly open in view of admiration and the absence of admiration. It is frequently observed that the best and ablest men are the most modest, and that very ordinary men are the most egotistical; that modesty and conceit are in inverse proportion to ability. But it is not as paradoxical as it seems. The modest man compares himself with those who are his superiors in attainments and achievements; the self-absorbed egotist compares himself with his inferiors, or with nobody at all. One compares himself upwards; the other compares himself downwards. One appreciates the talents and acquisitions of those who stand first, and is modest; the other compares himself (if he ever looks out from the closed circuit of his own thoughts and pursuits) with those who are, or who he fancies are, inferior to him, and is inflated with self-conceit. The Pharisee, who thanked God that he was not as other men are, compared himself, not with the best men of his time, not with Joseph of Arimathea the just counselor, nor with Nicodemus the honest seeker after truth, nor with John Baptist whose call to repentance the Pharisee must have heard, but with those who were worst or supposed to be worst, —

extortioners, adulterers, unjust, or yonder publican who presumes to come into the temple to pray. He did not lie, he did not cheat, he did not company with bad women, and he was not a publican. He compared himself downwards and was completely satisfied. The publican, who did not so much as lift his eyes towards heaven as he cried for mercy, had a vision of honesty and of purity, disclosed to him, no doubt, by some pure and honest soul. He measured himself upwards and was penitent. This is a parable, not only for religious standards, but also for intellectual and moral character. Egotism is wrapped up in its own insignificant self and despises others; modesty can admire superiority.

Modesty inspired with admiration sees and follows the line of improvement; egotism inflated with pride, self-sufficiency, and contempt, neither conceives nor desires improvement, but dwindles into yet smaller insignificance. "Seest thou a man wise in his own conceit? there is more hope of a fool than of him." The saying is true to fact; "every one that exalteth himself shall be abased, and he that humbleth himself shall be exalted." The ideals which humble also inspire and exalt. To have no ideals is to be abased, both in the estimation of others and in constant deterioration.

There is a wide difference between inspiration and imitation. Inspiration touches character — the

inner self.   Imitation touches externals — the outward man.   When Phillips Brooks was alive, scores
of young Episcopal clergymen tried to preach as
he did.   He had a habit of speaking rapidly (the
quick utterance being due to a tendency to stam-
mer), and of expanding his chest and spreading his
hands upon it.   So these young clergymen spoke
rapidly and expanded their chests and spread out
their hands.   They were putting on the garments
of the great preacher, imitating externals; but
the garments were too large, and hung very loosely
on the smaller men.   To many preachers, however,
Bishop Brooks was an inspiration.   Reality, genu-
ineness, freshness, sympathy, became the type of
preaching in hundreds of pulpits.   It may almost
be said that he changed the character of the American pulpit.

Admiration need not be servility.   Servile adulation places the great on an unapproachable
pinnacle, and obliterates self.   It widens distance.
True admiration inspires one to make similar attainments, to do kindred deeds, to have the same
character.   Democracy, on the whole, discourages
servility and promotes genuine admiration.   When
rank and class are impassable, besides those who
resent such artificial superiority are many who
become servile and obsequious.   When distinctions of rank and class do not exist, when char-

acter, culture, and achievement give superiority, when no gulf is fixed by externals, there is more of genuine admiration, more inspiration of example, less servility, and less resentment. It is thought that, in this country, wealth provokes hatred in some and servility in others, as hereditary rank does in other countries. There has been, and is, a sickening servility towards the rich. Many are eager to be introduced and to be on bowing (scarcely speaking) terms with the rich, although no possible advantage is to be derived from the acquaintance. But there seems to be some abatement of eager running after the wealthy. Enormous fortunes are looked upon with suspicion. We wonder how they were come by. For only a short time have we boasted that there are more millionaires in America than elsewhere. We now wish they were fewer. Mr. Howells remarks that it is not only the old-fashioned American who looks on wealth with misgiving, "it is the newest-fashioned American, the best educated, the most finely equipped, the young man choosing deliberately a high calling in which he cannot hope to make a fortune — it is he who regards the vast accumulations of money, once our admiration, with genuine contentment in his higher aim."[1] In another magazine, one writer says of the President of Co-

[1] "The Modern American Mood," *Harper's Magazine*, July, 1897.

lumbia University, whom many desire to see Mayor of Greater New York, that, although he is wealthy, he is never spoken of as a rich man, that the fact of his wealth "is obscured by the character, the spirit, the aim of the man, in truth by the man himself. In a time when great wealth excites so much comment, when the ignorant envy its owners, and some of the educated are devising schemes to check its accumulation and even to divide it, it is no small service to the public that one example should be set of wealth utterly forgotten in the personality of its possessor." [1] Now one false form of success and now another may be overvalued in popular estimation, yet in a democracy standards of intelligence and character have the best chance of winning admiration and creating inspiration. Such standards, embodied in superior persons, — in scholars, teachers, statesmen, artists, capitalists, and benefactors, — are the indispensable conditions of progress.

There is no danger that the supply of great men will give out, at any rate from lack of favorable circumstances. As against the prediction that there are not likely to be any more great men, because science can publish no discoveries comparable to those already made, because all the epic and dramatic situations have been exhausted, and

[1] Edward Cary, in *Review of Reviews*, July, 1897.

because the most momentous political changes are already accomplished, I have observed in an earlier work[1] that "it is rather rash to predict that there are to be no more distinguished statesmen while Bismarck and Gladstone are still living and are more widely famous than Pitt, or Burke, or Machiavelli were in their day; to affirm that there will be no more eminent scientific discoverers, considering that Darwin was unknown forty years ago; to prophesy that there will be no more great poets when it is remembered that the entire life of Tennyson and Browning was included in the present century. It might with equal force be argued that social discontent and democratic government furnish unprecedented conditions for leadership and fame; that national relations are so sensitive and the balance of power so delicate that, in use of the modern enginery of war, a soldier may yet appear more famous than any military genius of the past; that not all mysteries of nature are explored; that life does not cease to be dramatic because it is comfortable, but with refinement and culture becomes more sensitive, and so will give the poet ample material." Biologists believe that discoveries more important than any yet made await investigation of the germ-cell. It has been said that the next great philosophers and theologians must be accom-

---

[1] *Moral Evolution*, p. 47.

plished biologists. An entirely new school of poetry, making large use of the mechanism of railroads, deep-sea cables and ships, of cities, of commerce, and of modern labor has been founded in this decade by Kipling. National and international politics are on so large a scale that name and fame may be enhanced beyond any greatness of the past. Great movements require great leadership. General improvement and the diffusion of culture have not yet taken the place of great men who marshal and master the multitude. What would become of us if all were equally good and great, and we knew no superiors who inspire to noble deeds and feelings? What would become of us if all were equally small, sordid, and ignorant?

XVIII

THE PROGRESSION OF IDEALS

In a previous section attention was directed to the fact that progress is made by the consciousness of new wants, that the satisfaction of one want creates a fresh want which had been unforeseen. Now, new wants which one endeavors to realize are ideals. A want beyond experience is an ideal. Every one, in this sense, has ideals of some kind, material, intellectual, æsthetic, social, moral, religious, or a composite including some or all of those wants. There is one common characteristic of all those who pursue ideals and thereby make advancement. All do not have the same wants or ideals. Some are not capable of comprehending the ideals of others. A child does not understand his father's aims, thinks it a pity his father should waste time over dull books when he might be at play. A scholar's purposes are almost incomprehensible to an athlete. Who would be a dig when he might be a quarter-back? Social ambition is meaningless to an artist. The common characteristic is the *progression* of ideals. The satisfaction of one want creates another want, so that the ideal is always in advance. Unless one rests in a stagnant state, he is led on by some higher ideal, of the same sort, or of an entirely new sort.

The method of progression is also the same for all, whatever the ideal may be. The old ideal is not relinquished unless it is believed to be false and mistaken. The old ideal becomes customary, and upon it desire and effort reach out for the new and higher ideal. That which had been eagerly desired is so welded or woven into experience that it becomes familiar, customary, and almost automatic. This familiarizing of satisfied wants is worthy of careful notice.

Every one has had experience of novelties becoming commonplace. The most astonishing thing is the rapidity with which astonishing things become matter-of-course arrangements. Not long ago the beholder was amazed at the power of an electric wire to push heavily loaded cars through the streets. To-day he reads his newspaper as he is whirled along, and on every trip makes complaint of slowness and delay. The appliances of wealth, which are eagerly coveted by those who do not have them, are every-day conveniences to their possessors who give them scarcely a thought. Interest is transferred from the habitual to the unaccustomed. A carriage is simply a convenience, only an appliance to take its occupant to some place where he will do or enjoy something, simply a means to some other end. For pleasure he prefers a bicycle or his feet, and leaves his horses to eat off their heads in the stable. As the merchant drives through the park in an equipage perfectly appointed, the envy of pedestrians, he may be absorbed with the anxieties of business, or disturbed with thoughts of his dissipated and disappointing son, or planning a trip to Europe to be rid of the monotonous routine of his office, his daily drive, and his ten-course dinner, or impatient to reach home and take up the unfinished novel or to spend the evening at his club. His conveniences and luxuries actually become an encumbrance. His establishment brings more care than enjoyment. He thinks he envies the laborer who trudges homeward, puffing his pipe and swinging his empty dinner-pail. He perceives that contentment, like worth, is as likely to go on foot as in a high dogcart. His wife, poor thing, is at Aix-les-Bains, trying to recuperate from nervous prostration, brought on by entertaining, visiting, and the management of twenty servants.

The passage from old to new satisfactions may be called the extension of automatic action. A child learning to walk makes conscious effort with every uncertain step, and is delighted with his new accomplishment; but soon walking requires no conscious volition, is automatic, and when walking and running the child's mind is intent on flowers to be picked and games to be played. With painstaking effort the child learns to read. Every word is spelled out. But soon he is not aware of words and letters, but only of the thought expressed. Attention is not wanting, for a misspelt word and a misplaced letter is noticed. But the mind is liberated from the act of reading and concentrated on the object of reading. Playing the piano becomes automatic. The performer is not conscious of separate volitions as his fingers strike the keys. Attention is discharged from the mechanical act to the rhythm, harmony, and interpretation of the composition he renders. The exercise of nearly all physical and of many intellectual volitions which at first is conscious becomes automatic. Even moral actions may be so habitual as to become unconscious. The effect of this is not the restriction of voluntary by the extension of automatic action, but the liberation of volitional energy in new and higher directions. A man does not become a machine by changing the unaccustomed into the habitual. He only transfers choice and energy from a narrow to a wider circle. Even automatic is not necessitated action, for one can walk, read, add columns of figures, play a musical instrument, or not, as he chooses. To be sure, one can become an automaton. One can circle about in the narrow range of a few habits without seeking new experiences or making fresh attainments. To some it is painful to move out of the grooves of habitual action. They are the unmitigated conservatives, who get their growth early, and who would make an end of progress.

The extension of automatic action, instead of being a limitation, is the very condition of progress. The more languages one can read automatically, the more new knowledge one can acquire. The more automatic musical mechanics, the better appreciation of music, old and new. Were there no automatic action, humanity would be forever in leading strings and the alphabet, always beginning everything anew and making no progress. An ancient writer said that we are to leave first principles and go on unto perfection. He did not mean that first principles should be abandoned. He meant that first principles should be taken for granted, a second nature, and on that basis there should be advancement to new knowledge and finer character. Precisely so a boy should leave arithmetic and go on to geometry; arithmetic is not abandoned, but automatic facility in numbers conditions progress in the higher mathematics. This, now, is true of the economic, æsthetic, and moral life.   There is a progression of desires and ideals, and different persons are at different stages.   The step towards which this one is climbing, that one stands upon or has left beneath.   The coveted luxuries of some are the accustomed conveniences of others.   If income were doubled, one thinks one could be content.   But wants will double.   The first half will only give place and room for the satisfaction of other wants.   The laborer wants a better house.   The rich man has the house but wants to fill it with pictures and books.   The height of an instructor's ambition is to be a professor, but the professor wants to write books, to be made a member of the academy of science, to receive an honorary degree.   People might be grouped roughly according to their ideals ; some desiring what others already have, others aspiring to conditions which none have attained ; some embracing an ideal realized in material goods, others aiming at literary, æsthetic, philosophic, religious values ; and all, as they reach one vantage ground, stirred by desires for more of what they have, or for that which is different and better.   There is progression of ideals for each improving person, and there is an ascending scale of ideals for society.   The scale of ideals is determined partly by circumstance, but chiefly by personality.   The highest ideals may stir one who is in the lowest station.   The lowest ideals may appeal to one who is in the highest station. There are intelligent and refined workingmen and there are ignorant and coarse millionaires. Not, so many ideals corresponding to so many classes, but in every class, many men, many minds; and with all, progression from one ideal to another.

Contentment, therefore, is but slightly dependent on circumstances. Every one has observed this. In every condition some are contented and some are discontented. The amount of possessions seems to have nothing to do with contentment. A wage-earner is as contented and happy as his employer. I recall but do not remember a poem of Archbishop Trench's, to the effect that some murmur when a single cloud is in a clear sky and others are thankful for one patch of blue in the darkened heavens. Now, the accepted explanation of this well-known fact is not, I think, the correct, or, at least, is not the complete explanation. Contentment is due, it is usually said, to the spirit of the person and not to the abundance of the things he possesses, or, in philosophical terms, it is subjective, not objective. That is perfectly true, but the explanation assumes that a person of the right spirit is satisfied with what he has and asks for nothing more. But he is a very dull and stupid and despicable person who desires nothing more.

He has gone to seed. The correct definition is this : contentment is the gaining of the next satisfaction that is really desired. The workingman has some object which he wishes and expects to gain. He is trying to maintain a life insurance of two thousand dollars, or to carry his son through a textile school, or to buy his daughter a piano. See the contentment and delight of the man as he is attaining those objects. They are the natural extensions of his life. A rich man is contented if he is succeeding in a new venture, or secures a valuable picture which the connoisseurs have been trying to get, or if his son carries off the honors at graduation. His wife is contented if her diplomacy brings about a good match for her daughter, or if her paper on Browning is applauded by the literary sorosis. The pursuit and attainment of the objects which lie nearest in the path of life contribute reflexively to development of character. Certain virtues are cultivated in the workingman by his ambition for his family. Certain refinements of taste, a broader and keener sagacity, the pleasurable sense of success, are added to the personality of the merchant and the merchant's wife. Paul said that he had learned the secret in whatsoever state he was therewith to be content. It was because he learned that in any outward circumstance he could further the objects to which he was passionately devoted. When he was making tents he converted into Christians Priscilla and Aquila who worked at his side. When he was in prison at Rome he brought some soldiers of the pretorian guard into the Christian life, and wrote epistles which became part of the world's immortal literature. When he was shipwrecked he encouraged the frightened passengers, and was the means of saving two hundred and seventy-six persons. This same philosopher who was contented in any state also declared that he was always forgetting the things behind and reaching out for the things before, ever pressing towards the mark of the prize of a high calling. But that was the very reason he could be content in any outward circumstance. Contentment is anything but stagnation and repetition without desire for more. It is not, indeed, restless. It is serene, calm, and satisfied, just because it is ever reaching after and gaining some new and worthy end. It might be characterized as a state of moving equilibrium. A ship under sail is more steady than a ship at anchor. Zeno's illustration of the puzzle of motion and rest might be applied to the moving equilibrium of contentment in the progression of ideals. "The flying arrow rests," said Zeno, meaning that the swiftest motion is from one state of rest to another state of rest, or is successive states of rest; that nobody knows how a stationary body can get into motion nor how a moving body can stop moving. In quite another sense, a desire speeding to its aim is the desire of a restful and satisfied spirit. Aimlessness is restlessness. 'T is the flying arrow that rests. The American poet, John S. Dwight, well says : —

> " Rest is not quitting the busy career;
> Rest is the fitting of self to its sphere:
> 'T is the brook's motion, clear without strife,
> Fleeing to ocean after its life."

Contentment, then, is the continuous satisfaction of new wants. It is the second kind of discontent described in the sixteenth section. The discontent of ambition is the contentment of satisfying the new wants which grow out of old wants. The obvious reason for the disparity between circumstance and contentment is the different ambitions of different persons. The wants of one man are not the wants of another man, and so the two have different ambitions. A beggar does not want diamonds, though he may think he wants them. If he had them he would convert them into money and buy the things he really wants. The working-man does not want a masterpiece of Titian. If he had it he would sell it, and from the proceeds would buy a plot of land, build a snug little house, and mount his boys and girls on bicycles. He would realize his own ideals. Having become accustomed to them, he would desire other things which appeal to him according to the natural progression of his wants. He is contented in the gradual realization of ideals which the rich man long ago left behind and the scholar never had.

All who make progress, whatever possessions and attainments they already have, must put forth strenuous effort. They cannot saunter on, but must press on to the things which are before. In some sense, therefore, life is a struggle, certainly for all who make appreciable progress, and no one should expect or desire to escape it. Our sympathies are excited by the hardships of laborers who are deprived of many comforts. If we knew the hardships and self-denials of scores of instructors in the great universities, we might be equally sympathetic. The instructor has a family, and his salary is small. He must live in a respectable house near the university, must dress decently, must maintain his family in keeping with their social position, must have books, and must respond to many calls of associations and clubs. Such men and their wives have more anxiety about ways and means than the majority of workingmen have. But they practice the denials cheerfully, because they prefer their work and life to any other. They are neither complaining nor envious. They do not ask for sympathy. If a man has an ideal which is worthy, we do not pity his hardships and struggles unless he is actually suffering.

Every man that can earn his living has some vantage ground from which he can reach the higher values. Those values are not the same for all. One does not need to follow all the tracks of another. One earns wealth and has the discipline of his labor. Another inherits wealth and has the discipline of study and culture. Still another devotes his energies to teaching or preaching, with small compensation, rather than to mechanical or mercantile pursuits. The circumstance, after all, is the least of it. Life, indeed, may be made too easy. Comfortable and luxurious circumstances may spoil character as certainly as indiscriminate charity may pauperize able-bodied men and women. "Even in a palace one may live well;" but the observation marks a great difficulty. The constant preachment that more should be done for working people may lead them to despise the possibilities that are open to their own thrift and ambition. The severest hardship is absence of some incentive of necessity.

Let every one always be making advancement from what is to what may be, according to his own circumstances and ability. We need not compare ourselves with others, but each should compare his actual self with his ideal self, and follow the progression of his own true and right ambitions. Professor Jowett, after he was sixty years old, frequently said that he was always making fresh beginnings. " I always seem to be beginning life again, and may I ever seem to be beginning life again until the end! I have always the feeling that I have lost so much time that I can never have a holiday. I trust that during the last ten years I may work only from the highest motives." Among various maxims to be followed on the approach of age, by a man of sixty years, one is: " He may truly think of the last years of life as the best, and of every year as better than the last, if he knows how to use it." [1]

[1] *Life and Letters*, vol. ii. pp. 79, 111.

XIX

UNIQUENESS AND UNITY

In these days much complaint is made about the separation and antagonism of classes in society, and effort is directed towards the unifying of men. To superficial observation equalizing seems the condition of unity. It is thought that the more nearly alike men are in circumstances and culture the closer will be their union. But, in fact, unity depends on unlikeness. Things which are alike are in juxtaposition; things which are unlike unite to form a whole. Union of equals is a process in addition; union of unequals is a process in multiplication. The Hegelian philosophy finds the unity of society in the uniqueness of individuals. The perfect society would consist of perfect individuals, each self-centred and unique. One writer says, in comment, " If, on one side, we are defective at present because we are not joined closely enough together, we are defective, on the other side, because we are not sufficiently differentiated apart." [1]

[1] Professor J. Ellis McTaggart, *The International Journal of Ethics*, July, 1897.

This relation has been suggested in previous sections, but is now re-stated in another form, and with the advantage of the considerations concerning variety which have been perceived.

The most unique men are the most universal in relations and sympathies. Shakespeare stands alone in intellectual greatness. There is only one Shakespeare. But his distinction is his humanness. He sounds the entire gamut of human thoughts, hopes, fears, and passions. He is universal. A German theologian finds the unparalleled power of Jesus in the unlimited range of his sympathies. He stands apart from and above all men in greatness. He is absolutely unique. He is, as Bushnell said, unclassifiable. But is not his uniqueness this, that he is not provincial, local, and narrow, but universal; that he knew what is in man as no other has known, and that he had power of sympathetic union with men and women of any nation and any religion? He whose uniqueness made him the Son of God was he whose universality made him the Son of man. Dr. Dorner therefore lays down the principle that the uniqueness of Jesus is his universality. The greatness and distinction of any person is measured by his sympathetic range. An educated negro who recently read "Uncle Tom's Cabin" for the first time, told me that he was most struck with Mrs.

Stowe's knowledge of the feelings and thoughts of people belonging to another race. The universal popularity of the book reveals the unique power of the writer. It is said that Hugh Miller, the geologist, could adapt himself to all sorts of people; that he would trudge along the high-road with a workingman, and make the man feel that he was conferring a favor on the great geologist by the companionship. Paul had his limitations. He was a Hebrew of the Hebrews, and showed that he was in every letter he wrote. But he was broad enough to accommodate the presentation of truth to Jews and Greeks, to masters and slaves, to the strong and the weak. It was no reproach that he was all things to all men, but was a mark of versatility and greatness. He was unique in the possession of that very power. A small, commonplace man, without unique characteristics, is one thing to all men. He is read at a glance. He shows his one side, or perchance two sides, to every one on first acquaintance. This is true of men as they actually are: that the small men, who are nearly alike, have fewest points of union with others; that the great men, who are unlike, have many points of union with others; that the unity of society is conditioned on the uniqueness of unlike individuals, and that unity is therefore the very opposite of homogeneity and uniformity.

We may now advance a step farther in the same direction. As society makes progress, individuals become more, not less unique. The higher unity is a more complex variety. We therefore perceive that the ideals of persons are more unique than the actual persons; that, if individuals should become their true and best selves, they would be more and more original in distinctive uniqueness. This tendency can be marked in observed improvement and retrogression. As persons go down the scale they become alike. Vice, for example, tends to sameness. It degrades, we say; that is, it grades down. A gallery of rogues, while the faces are somewhat unlike, shows the same coarse, sinister, brutal expression in all the pictures. On the other hand, a gallery of fair women presents variety of type. You look at one face and exclaim with delight. You look at another face and exclaim again with delight. Yet they are very unlike. One is all smiles, sweetness, gracefulness; the other is all dignity, reserve, graciousness. Vice and ignorance tend to sameness; beauty and virtue tend to variety. If, now, this should be followed out, it would be seen, as I said, that the ideals of persons, their perfect selves, are more unlike than the actual selves; that, as each develops according to his own type, he becomes more, not less, distinctive. Whatever the uniqueness of any person, it will be developed to the utmost; and everybody, after all, is unique in some respect. Dr. Holmes said that the most commonplace life has material enough to make a three-volume novel. In fact, one school of novelists makes interesting stories by photographing with fidelity the most commonplace characters, on the assumption that there are vast possibilities in every life. Let those possibilities be realized, and ordinary persons would have unique interest and charm. Every one, if you please, is an original idea of God's. He sees the man in the child, the ideal man in the actual man; and he does not repeat himself. We see that idea, each for himself, as we study our tastes and aptitudes, as we choose and succeed in the pursuits which are congenial, as we cultivate ourselves along the lines of our characteristics and endowments. Here is the truth of the old doctrine of Creationism. It is the doctrine that each soul coming into the world is a fresh and immediate creation of God's. The belief was entertained when heredity was not as well understood as it is now. But the truth for which the doctrine stood is apparent in the diversity of individuals, even of those who have the same heredity. A curious notion of a French writer, Godet, is the fancy that there are three grades of beings, — animals, men, and angels, — which are distinguished by the relative degrees of heredity and individuality. Animals, he thinks, are almost exact reproductions of their kind. The species is continued with but slight variations. Men are under the laws of heredity, but individuality is more marked. Angels, who neither marry nor are given in marriage, are not the products of heredity, but are direct creations of distinct individuality. Such a view, although fanciful, has a certain justification in the observed facts of differentiated human nature, and in the tendency of progress to make persons more and more unlike. When we reach our ideals (symbolized as angels in heaven), each of us will be perfectly unique. There will be no monotony in heaven. But ideal persons, like the angels of God, will be all the more capable of intellectual and sympathetic union with one another. There is more joy in the presence of pure and spotless angels than in the presence of impure and tainted men over a sinner that repenteth.

Unity, then, is anything but uniformity. It is possible only in variety, and is realized through the reciprocal functions of differentiated persons. Nothing is so tiresome as unbroken uniformity, whether it is seven English sisters dressed exactly alike, or Chinese music drummed out on tom-toms, or an interminable plain traversed for weeks on horseback or even for days on a railway train, or any other unvarying repetition. Nothing is so pleasing as unity and harmony in variety. In dress, variety and contrast reflect good taste. It will be a grateful relief when the evening dress of gentlemen exhibits diversity, as already morning costumes allow knickerbockers and colors. Music exists by combinations and contrasts, even by occasional discords. Flowers and music are as unlike as the eye and the ear which perceive them, yet go so well together that certain tones suggest certain flowers, or at least certain colors, to some minds. Travelers on the plains rejoice when they pass among mountains and skirt the banks of rivers.

Uniqueness, of course, depends on unity with others as truly as unity depends on variety. The health of every member and the health of the whole organism depend on the exercise of the appropriate function of each organ in giving and receiving. The hand is a distinct and wonderful member of the body; but a hand severed from the arm is a hand no longer; it must receive from the whole body and do its work in the body to be a hand at all; and the body deprived of the hand is maimed and incomplete. The leaf of a rose after it is pulled out is not a living leaf, but is already decomposing as it falls from your hand to the ground; and the rose minus a single leaf is an imperfect flower with all its petals loosened. So a man is not a true man unless he is in vital relation with his fellow men in the great social body of many members, in the consummate flower of a symmetrical humanity with its manifold and different functions.

It is the middle term of the eighteenth century watchword which needs revision, and the middle term only. Had it been liberty, inequality, fraternity, or liberty, individuality, fraternity, it might not have been resonant enough for popular shouting and echo, but the first and third terms would have had some chance of realization. Inequality without liberty and fraternity is indeed an evil. But essential equality would destroy personal freedom, and would leave as much fraternity as a man enjoys when he looks at himself in a mirror. Liberty and fraternity are possible only through the variety of coördination and reciprocity, which is anything but equality. Real freedom is enjoyed when one has scope for the exercise of one's own individual powers, as a machine plays freely when it acts according to the peculiar law of its structure, and labors when it is geared to connections too great or too small for its service of foot-pounds. Fraternity is mutual service in variety of functions, from interchange of commodities to interchange of thought. The exchange of ten bushels of wheat for ten bushels of wheat is not commerce. Economic reciprocity is exchange of ten bushels of wheat for a coat. Inequality is the middle term which gives personal liberty on one side and social fraternity on the other side. Liberty and fraternity, like peace and righteousness, meet together and kiss each other when every one exercises his peculiar gift in service of production and in reception of the various service of others. The gift itself is developed in its use for others. In selfish use of power there can be no greatness. Liberty is gained by rendering the largest service willingly. Thus there is scope for development and a career is opened to talents. Conversely, the very consciousness and exercise of ability in promoting the common welfare and happiness strengthen the fraternal spirit. Thus the highest unity is the reciprocity of unique individuals.

XX

CHRISTIANITY AND INEQUALITY

DEMOCRACY and Christianity have, in important respects, a common task: to secure to every individual his right, to realize for every individual his worth. Both reach out and reach down to the lowest, so that every man shall be integral part of the whole. Democracy makes every man a citizen. Christianity makes every man a member of the kingdom of God. No one residing within the limits of a nation is to be excluded from the rights and privileges of citizenship. No one within the limits of humanity is to be excluded from the realization of his own worth. Regarded as citizens or as children of God, all men are essentially equal. There are common experiences of affection, sympathy, sorrow, faith, as there is a common loyalty of all citizens in a nationality. On this basis men are much alike. The grief of a laborer who stands by the dead body of his child commands the respect and sympathy of his employer who knows the same experience and who silently presses the hand of the sufferer. "One touch of nature makes the whole

world kin." A great company of worshipers are
stirred by the same emotions. One speaker, pre-
senting the high themes, the duties and the aspira-
tions of religion, sways the minds of a thousand
listeners as if they were one person, as an orator
moves a vast audience of the most dissimilar individuals by appeal to patriotism. The sculptor de-
picts the very same emotion and purpose on the
dusky faces of negro soldiers as he brings out on
the determined countenance of their cultivated
commander. In one sense, and perhaps the largest sense, democracy stands for the basal equality
of all citizens. In one sense, and perhaps the
largest sense, Christianity stands for the immortal
worth of all men as children of God and brethren
in one family.

These interests of democracy and of Christianity are among the great interests of humanity.
When the aims and progress of democracy are
perceived they seem to be occupied with the equality of citizens. The gospel, in one view of it, has
the one aim of bringing all men equally to their
right and worth. Concerning all this there need
be, there can be, no question. It would be interesting to follow the course of democracy reclaim-
ing to citizenship man after man, class after class;
and to follow Christianity as it has given slaves
their freedom and women their equal place with

men, as it has gone down and out to the heathen, the outside peoples, to every class, rank, condition, with its one great sufficient, human salvation, creating the holy church throughout all the world; and to recognize the mutual action of Christianity and democracy in their universalizing work. These facts, with which we started, are repeated that there may be no mistake concerning the equalities and the inequalities of men.

But the universalizing function of these two great moral powers is not undiscriminating. They do not profess to make all men equal in all respects. Both emphasize the variety of human endowments and functions, as giving the possibility of national and of Christian unity. Democracy brings the strong into the service of the weak, and thus is able to raise the lowest man. It dethrones an aristocracy which exists only to exact the service and homage of the weak. It impresses the best talents into the service of the State, and requires of the least their support and the product of their industry. It would not and cannot do away with distinctions of great and less, but makes greatness the measure of service, while it excuses no man from the little he can do because it is little. Thus it promotes civilization and guarantees its own perpetuity. A nation is a unity in variety, not an interminable series of identical men.

It is the language of Christianity which has just been applied with entire appropriateness to democracy. Jesus had almost as much to say about the differences as about the common salvation of men. He spoke of those who are great, but gave no intimation that they ought to reduce their superiority to a common level. The use and misuse of greatness were his only concern. The great ones among the nations lorded it over the inferior. " It shall not be so among you," Jesus said to his disciples. But he did not say that they were to abdicate such greatness as they had. They were to use it in ministration to those who, because they need such service, are not great. On the other hand, the widow is not to withhold her mite because it is not equal to the wealth of those who cast in of their abundance. The woman who anointed Jesus' feet was commended because she did what she could. There was no measure, in either case, of less or more, but only the measure of ability. The parable of the talents is based on the unequal endowments of men, and the man who came under condemnation was the man who did not use the little he had. The parable of the pounds is based on the unequal use of equal endowments. All had the same amount, one pound each, but increments varied from ten pounds to nothing. Both these parables, which are probably different reports of the same parable, emphasize inequality; one in respect to endowment, the other in respect to increment. Both, therefore, are true to life, for men are unequal not only in native ability, but also in the use of the same talents. Faithfulness to one's own self in use of what one has is the lesson of both parables.

Paul teaches explicitly that unity consists in variety. The members of the body are not only numerous but also are different, and in the differences or variety is the unity. So the Church is one body of many members. All grades and kinds of power are enumerated, from apostleship down to any least helpfulness, such as hospitality. Moreover, peculiar gifts are developed in their peculiarity by exercise in the great united society, and in ministration to the diverse needs of mankind. Every gift or function is to be exercised in its own best and peculiar way: giving is to be with simplicity of motive; mercy is to be shown with cheerfulness; prophecy, that is preaching, is to be according to the proportion of faith, not less nor more than the preacher really believes; and love is to be without dissimulation. Each characteristic gift is to be exercised characteristically. No man is to think of himself more highly than he ought to think, but is to think of himself soberly, that is, correctly, neither overestimating nor underestimat-

ing himself. Every member is humbled by the
knowledge that he is only a single part of the
great social unity, but in that many-sided relation
his power of service is multiplied by many other
factors. These discriminating and inspiring con-
ceptions flow forth from and flow back into the
one noble conception of unity in variety, which has
a concise and suggestive expression unsurpassed in
literature: "For even as we have many members
in one body, and all the members have not the
same office: so we, who are many, are one body
in Christ, and severally members one of another."
Unity in variety is a favorite thought of the apostle. He impresses it on almost every church to
which he writes. The thought is so true and so
characteristic of Christianity at work that I cannot refrain from quoting entire another fine passage: "Now there are diversities of gifts, but the
same Spirit. And there are diversities of minis-
trations, and the same Lord. And there are diversities of workings, but the same God, who worketh
all things in all. But to each one is given the
manifestation of the Spirit to profit withal. For
to one is given through the Spirit the word of
wisdom; and to another the word of knowledge,
according to the same Spirit: to another faith, in
the same Spirit; and to another gifts of healings,
in the one Spirit; and to another workings of

miracles; and to another prophecy; and to another discernings of spirits: to another divers kinds of tongues; and to another the interpretation of tongues: but all these worketh the one and the same Spirit, dividing to each one severally even as he will." Why are men so different, so unequal? Why is one an apostle, and another only a healer? That question will never be answered. The Spirit divides to each one severally, even as He will. But otherwise there would be dull, tame, monotonous uniformity, instead of beautiful, harmonious unity. So the healer heals and the apostle preaches. The law of earth is the law of the heavens. As there is a terrestrial so there is a celestial unity in variety. There is one glory of the sun, and another glory of the moon, and another glory of the stars; for one star differeth from another star in glory. So also is the resurrection of the dead.

Nowhere in the New Testament is there the faintest intimation that the kingdom on earth or in heaven is to be composed of persons who were made equal or have become equal. In fact, there is to be release from the apparent and artificial samenesses by which men had been classified in nations and classes, and individuality is to have its perfect and ample development through knowledge, faith, hope, and love. Class, caste, sex, and nationality are not the distinctive marks; but the individual stands out, his own unique self, making the most and the best of himself, after the pattern of Christ, and through the reciprocities of Christian unity in variety. The higher unity transcends the lower unity. "There can be neither Jew nor Greek, there can be neither bond nor free, there can be no male and female; for ye all are one man in Christ Jesus." And yet, the higher sympathetic unity does not destroy the lower unities of nationality, sex, class, and kindred tastes. The seer on Patmos had a vision of the perfected, harmonious society, standing before a great throne and with one voice, as the voice of many waters, ascribing salvation to God. He observed that they were out of every nation, and of all tribes and peoples and tongues. Characteristic marks of nationality and speech remained. He does not say that they once belonged to different nations and tribes, but had become indistinguishable. He noticed the differences and reported them. The universal kingdom was seen to be a unity in variety.

A very good argument could be made to the effect that the doctrine of election is the calling of nations and individuals to the exercise of their peculiar functions. The elect are the select — those selected according to fitness for their place and work in that kingdom which is universal, because it is capacious of all gifts, endowments, and talents in the reciprocal services of knowledge and of love.

The opinions which have been advanced in this volume are, I believe, in the main correct. They have been fortified by facts drawn from many sources. I said at the start that I am not concerned about the applications of my conclusions to social schemes. All social theories must reckon with the almost infinite diversity of human nature. The impulse at the heart of socialism is a good and humane impulse. So is the impulse at the heart of individualism. Some so-called socialists, when they pass from the general to the specific, admit the facts which have been pointed out, and are scarcely to be distinguished from those who oppose and deride socialism. All, by whatever name they may be called, all who would promote the welfare and advancement of their fellow men, should reduce the unknown quantities of large social equations to the lowest concrete terms. The inequality of variety is not merely a stubborn fact which must be set over against vague notions of equality, nor is it simply the inevitable against which it is useless to contend. It is a fact to be welcomed, a fact on which the hope of progress firmly rests.

From first to last this essay has been simply an illustration of that variety which gives the harmonious, sympathetic, and mutually helpful unity of men.

The Riverside Press

CAMBRIDGE, MASSACHUSETTS, U. S. A.
ELECTROTYPED AND PRINTED BY
H. O. HOUGHTON AND CO.

LargePrintLiberty.com

Dedicated to offering books on libertarian thought and economics in Large Print paperback.

Titles include:

For a New Liberty, by Murray N. Rothbard (Philosophy)
"A classic that for over two decades has been hailed as the best general work on libertarianism available. Rothbard begins with a quick overview of its historical roots, and then goes on to define libertarianism as resting 'upon one single axiom: that no man or group of men shall aggress upon the person or property of anyone else.' He writes a withering critique of the chief violator of liberty: the State. Rothbard then provides penetrating libertarian solutions for many of today's most pressing problems, including poverty, war, threats to civil liberties, the education crisis, and more."

Principles of Economics, by Carl Menger (Economics)
"In the beginning, there was Menger. It was this book that reformulated, and really rescued, economic science. It kicked off the Marginalist Revolution, which corrected theoretical errors of the old classical school. These errors concerned value theory, and they had sown enough confusion to make the dangerous ideology of Marxism seem more plausible than it really was. Menger set out to elucidate the precise nature of economic value, and root economics firmly in the real-world actions of individual human beings."

Great Wars and Great Leaders, by Ralph Raico (History)
"In the backdrop of this blistering and deeply insightful and scholarly history is the whitewashing of 'great leaders' like Woodrow Wilson, Winston Churchill, FDR, Truman, Stalin, Trotsky, and other collectivists. They are highly regarded because they were on the 'right side' of the rise of the state. But do they deserve adulation? Raico says no: these great leaders were main agents in the decline of civilization in the 20th century, all of them anti-liberals who used their power to celebrate and enhance state power."

www.ingramcontent.com/pod-product-compliance
Lightning Source LLC
Chambersburg PA
CBHW081102290526
45795CB00006B/1960